BY THE NUMBERS : USING DEMOGRA

By the Numbers

By the Numbers
Using Demographics and Psychographics for Business Growth in the '90s

Judith E. Nichols, CFRE

BONUS BOOKS, INC.

Library of Congress Catalog Card Number:
90-82405

International Standard Book Number:
0-929387-45-7

Bonus Books, Inc.
160 East Illinois Street
Chicago, Illinois 60611

94   93   92   91   90   5   4   3   2   1

Printed in the United States of America

Contents

INTRODUCTION

BY THE NUMBERS: *Using Demographics and Psychographics for Business Growth in the '90s* will show you how to use what's happened and what's coming in the final decade of the twentieth century to make your business successful.

This is a "how-to" book. It is filled with practical advice and suggestions on strategies you can use to keep your business competitive through the 1990s. I am grateful to my many colleagues and friends who have generously shared their experiences with me and helped to shape my thinking on the subject.

By the Numbers is divided into five sections:

Part 1: Understanding Changing Demographics and Psychographics is a commonsense introduction to the subject, and suggests where you can get more in-depth information in a usable format.

Part 2: Building Your Consumer Base in the 1990s outlines the key trends—Baby Boomers, the Hispanic "Majority," Aging America, and Working Women— and demonstrates how to target your marketing efforts to reach them effectively and efficiently. You'll also meet the Baby Busters, whose muscle will begin flexing around the mid-1990s.

Part 3: Picking the Better Business Niches of the 1990s offers some predictions as to what businesses will succeed in the next ten years and why. The key niches—the home, education, health, leisure, and financial services—are explored in marketing terms.

Part 4: Planning Your Marketing Strategy for the 1990s
takes mass and face-to-face marketing in new directions, showing how partnerships with not-for-profits are adding a new dimension for businesses.

Part 5: Keeping Your Business Healthy in the 1990s gives
important advice on who will lead and who will work in the
businesses of the nineties, and includes a closing chapter on
looking ahead to the twenty-first century.

By the Numbers grew out of requests I received to apply
the principles I used in my first book, *Changing Demographics: Fund Raising in the 1990s* (Bonus Books, 1990), to the
wider business community. Small businesses will find this to
be a similar "bible," that will walk them through a business
strategy driven by demographics and psychographics. And it
will serve as a reminder to large corporations as to just where
their customers will come from in the new decade.

This book contains a lot of quotes from a lot of people and
journals and research firms. The most meaningful are included so that readers do not have to rediscover the wheel and
check a wide range of resources. That's been done for you. If
you'd like more information on a concept or an observation,
the citations are provided to let you dig into the original research. For the most part, though, what is provided is all that
you really need to understand the changes that will affect your
business or your mission.

PART I

UNDERSTANDING CHANGING
DEMOGRAPHICS AND PSYCHOGRAPHICS

Harold (Bud) Hodgkinson, a noted educator and demographics expert, asserts that "demography is destiny." Hodgkinson says that today's four-year-olds will do one simple but important thing: They will grow up to become tomorrow's adults. That is a demographic certainty.

He lists four underlying demographic truths:

The more people that are born in the same year as you, the harder you must compete for resources and recognition. This has shaped the lives of the **baby boomers**, 76 million people born between 1946 and 1964.

Some people have more children than others and, thus, will be overrepresented in future populations. While the average white American is 31 years of age and the average black American is 26, the average **Hispanic American** is just 22. By the year 2010, one-third of the under-eighteen U.S. population will be minority—the bulk of it Hispanic.

Some people live a lot longer than other people. **America is aging.** Today, there are 29 million older Americans. By 1990, there will be 32 million. By 2000, there will be 35 million. By 2020, nearly one of every five Americans will be older than 65. This is the *senior boom*.

The number of children born to single people and people over the age of sixty-five tends to be low. The entry of **women into the workforce** beginning with the years of World War II has contributed dramatically to changing birth patterns. It has been called "the single most significant societal trend of the twentieth century."

The four major societal trends—Baby Boomers, the Emerging Hispanic Majority, the Aging of America, and the Growth of Women in the Workforce—will significantly affect not only the purchasing patterns of individuals, dramatically altering who buys what and where the potential is for successful new products and services, but also who will offer these products and services, and where available funding can be found for these newly emerging businesses.

Before we can explore who your customers and consumers will be in the 1990s, and how to reach them, you'll need to understand the concepts behind demographics, geo-demographics, and psychographics. Chapters 1, 2, and 3 teach you the basics. Chapter 4 will show you where to turn for the tools to use these concepts effectively.

CHAPTER ONE

A Quick Lesson on Demographics

THIS CHAPTER WILL "set the stage" for the material in *By the Numbers* by introducing some basic information.

First, some definitions:

- **Demographics** are sets of characteristics about people that relate to their behavior as consumers. Age, sex, race, marital status, education, and income are used most frequently. Because marketers rarely focus on a single person, we look for such similarities so we can mass market to groups of individuals.

- **Geo-demographics** integrates population and geographic characteristics—specifically relating to a particular population and its location, such as a neighborhood—into demographics.

- **Segmentation** divides a large population into smaller groups with like characteristics. To make demographic and geo-demographic information useful for markets, we segment.

- **Psychographics** are the measure of attitudes, values, or lifestyles. Taken from surveys and observations, they can be integrated with demographic measures to put "flesh" on an individual or group of persons.

INTRODUCING TARGETED MARKETING

Once we know who, demographically, our target individuals or groups are, we want to know and understand, psychographically, what makes that one individual or group act the same as or differently from another.

To effectively build an expanded and upgraded consumer base, marketers need to use **targeted marketing**—combining geographic, demographic, and psychographic consumer attributes—to impact consumer behavior.

**Elements of Consumer Segmentation
and Targeting (Consumer Attributes)***

- **Geographic**
  Regional cultural/economic
  Census geography
  Non-census geography

- **Demographic**
  Age, sex, race
  Education, occupation, income
  Household characteristics
  Residence
  Life cycle

- **Psychographic**
  Social values and beliefs
  Attitudes, interests, opinions
  Lifestyles
  Benefits

*As defined by American Demographics Institute.

Using the full range of elements of consumer segmentation and targeting (consumer attitudes) allows us to most effectively influence consumer behavior.

Earlier, I indicated that four major societal trends—Baby Boomers, the Emerging Hispanic Majority, the Aging of America, and the Growth of Women in the Workforce—will significantly alter the 1990s. Demographics can explain why this is so.

WHO'S GOT THE DOLLARS? LOOKING DEMOGRAPHICALLY AT ECONOMICS.

Almost 70 percent of total income growth between 1985 and 2000 will be accounted for by the 35 to 50 age group. And the age group 45 to 55 will more than double its spending power by the year 2000. This is the **Baby Boom.**

While the age group of 25 to 35 has a below-average household income (understandably so, because many of them are just entering the workforce), they account for 22 percent of total income. The emerging **Hispanic Majority** is heavily represented among this group of younger Americans.

When we look at who has discretionary income, we target Americans age 50 and over. **Aging America** is growing more rapidly than any other group in our society.

Who has the spending power? Roughly, 80 percent of the $50,000 and over income bracket households are made up of two or more wage earners, caused by the growth of **Women in the Workforce.**

Now that you know why the four major trends are important in demographic terms, let's learn how to use geodemographics to find Baby Boomers, Hispanic Americans, Older Americans, Working Women, or any other group you need to target.

CHAPTER TWO

Refining with Geo-demographics

HERE WE'LL LEARN how to use demographic tools to do a better job of identifying, screening, and researching who your customers are, and who your prospects are likely to be.

A BIT OF HISTORY

In the early 1980s, a myriad of information describing the U.S. population was made available by the Census Bureau in a relatively inexpensive and very accessible computer tape format. With this inexpensive database on hand, market researchers began to expand their markets by promising corporations a new, more extensive, quicker, and cheaper method for targeting their sales markets. Although target marketing was not new, the ability to quickly analyze massive amounts of data with sophisticated computerized programs, taking into account behavior patterns as well as demographic data such as income, home value, education level, etc., allowed for a variety of new uses for this type of marketing. Today, marketers can use lifestyles *plus* demographics to target high potential prospects. This process of segmentation is called **geo-demographics.**

To segment effectively, you must be able to identify, quantify, and locate homogeneous market segments. The power of geo-demographics is that it will locate that homogeneous market segment that a marketer feels most closely matches his/her product or service.

WHAT IS GEO-DEMOGRAPHICS?

To understand geo-demographics, you need to understand geography. Daniel F. Hansler* offers this explanation:

> The United States is made up of 50 states and over 300 metropolitan statistical areas, called MSA's. States and MSA's are broken down into counties. Counties are broken down into postal geography and census geography. There are approximately 42,000 zip codes with an average of 2,150 households per zip code. This average can be misleading since the average zip code in a metropolitan area contains over 6,000 households. There are over 200,000 carrier routes.
>
> Counties are also divided into census tracts and major civil divisions. There are approximately 69,000 of these units in the United States with an average population of 1,300 households. Finally, census tracts and minor civil divisions are divided into block groups. There are over 250,000 of these units in the United States with an average of 361 households. This is the lowest level of census geography (covering the smallest area and containing the least population) for which detailed census data is released.
>
> These "block groups" are the neighborhoods that are the basis of a geo-demographic segmentation system. Since the neighborhoods have a geographic reference (latitude and longitude) they can be easily identified and subsequently located. Now add to this identifiable geographic location, demographic data and census data, as well as buying habits and responses to surveys, and one can build a rather comprehensive composite view of a neighborhood.
>
> It has been demonstrated that your home address (where you live) largely reflects how you live. You are where you live. Since the geo-demographic neighborhoods contain only approximately 361 homes there is a high degree of homogeneity in these neigh-

---

*President of The Fund Raising Marketing Company, Inc., Concord, California.

borhoods. It has also been demonstrated that these neighborhoods are replicated all over the country. In other words, a certain type of upscale suburban neighborhood near San Francisco has the same demographics and exhibits similar behavior to certain other upscale suburban neighborhoods near Chicago, Dallas, Atlanta, etc.

As government census data presentations became more sophisticated and the power of the computer was harnessed, the segmenting systems became more and more complex. By the mid-1980s, a whole new generation of geo-demographic clustering systems were developed. They combined census data, individual databases and consumer behavior to develop segmentation systems designed to predict household behavior, rather than infer it. With this ability, geo-demographics became a useful tool for marketers.

GEO-DEMOGRAPHIC SCREENING TOOLS

A number of geo-demographic systems are available. All work in similar fashion. Information on National Decision Systems was furnished by Daniel Hansler. Other systems are listed in Chapter 4, along with demographic and psychographic resources.

■ **National Decision Systems: VISION™**
In the 1970s, National Decision Systems pioneered the use of geo-demographics. VISION™ is the second generation of NDS's research. VISION™ classifies every household in the United States into one of forty-eight market segments based on the demographic, socioeconomic and housing characteristics of its neighborhood block group. Each market segment is defined so that consumption, purchasing, and financial behavior is very homogeneous within the market segment, but very different from the other segments. Over one hundred variables are used in this computerized classification.

   Households are segmented, then clustered. The first division of the forty-eight segments relates to the type of residential area they represent. They are:

```
S  -  Suburban
U  -  Urban
T  -  Towns
R  -  Rural
```

These areas are then segmented by general affluence:

```
U  -  Very high socioeconomic status
H  -  High socioeconomic status
M  -  Middle socioeconomic status
L  -  Low socioeconomic status
```

By combining these areas and general affluence group-ings, VISION™ is grouped into twelve categories:

```
 1. Suburban Wealthy
 2. Urban Affluence
 3. Suburban Affluence
 4. Suburban Middle Class
 5. Urban Middle Class
 6. Town Middle Class
 7. Rural Middle Class
 8. Suburban Lower Income
 9. Urban Lower Income
10. Town Lower Income
11. Rural Lower Income
12. Special Populations
```

The twelve categories are divided into forty-eight market segments, not listed here. To make these forty-eight VISION™ segments a little easier to distinguish, each has a descriptive label or nickname, such as "Suburban Gentry," "Young Urban Professionals," "Carports and Kids," and "Prairie People." Two VISION™ segments are described in some detail:

SUBURBAN GENTRY

SU1 Market

Segment	Wealthy, Older Suburbs, Professionals
DEMOGRAPHICS	White Families, Teens, Empty Nesters
SOCIOECONOMIC	Highest Income in U.S., Old and New Money, Highly Educated Professional Class
HOUSING	Single Family Suburban Housing, Very High Value
LOCATION	America's Top Metropolitan Areas
LIFESTYLE	Big spenders and big savers. **High** on investment, expensive travel and leisure activities, theatre, restaurants, liquor, magazines, books, large expensive cars, tuition, teenage sports, and home electronic equipment. **Low** on household durables and furniture, fast food, and do-it-yourself items.

YOUNG URBAN PROFESSIONALS

<u>UU5</u> Market

Segment	Urban Professionals, Singles/Couples, High Income
DEMOGRAPHICS	Young, White Collar, Singles and Couples, College Educated
SOCIOECONOMIC	High Income, Two-Income Households
HOUSING	Condos, Townhomes, High Rent, High Value
LOCATION	America's Top Cities
LIFESTYLE	Big spenders and low savers. **High** on electronic equipment, restaurants, theatre, movies, clothing, outdoor recreation activities, magazines and books. **Low** on grocery and children's products, TV viewing, large cars. Big users of credit cards and direct mail.

Birds of a feather flock together. The fundamental axiom of geo-demographic systems is that households in a neighborhood share similar lifestyles; and that these neighborhoods repeat themselves across the United States, so that similar neighborhoods can be classified into a smaller number of market segments.

Geo-demographic services can provide report formats that give marketers the population, housing, and income information necessary to:

- Identify new markets that match your customer profile to pinpoint expansion opportunities.
- Analyze the demographic changes that impact the success of your existing sites.
- Identify specific geographic areas that meet your marketing criteria.
- Develop marketing, advertising and sales plans that target the people residing within a defined market.
- Conduct feasibility studies.
- Quickly compare one market to another.
- Demonstrate the market potential of a site when selling or leasing property.

Simply—Using geo-demographics can help marketers answer four key questions:

■ Who are my best customers?

■ Where and how do they live?

■ What do they read, listen to, and watch?

■ How can I reach them most effectively?

CHAPTER THREE

Adding Psychographics

DEMOGRAPHICS GIVES YOU AN understanding of larger-scale similarities and trends; **psychographics,** according to Arnold Mitchell, who originated the psychographic approach to market segmentation, describes "the entire constellation of a person's attitudes, beliefs, opinions, hopes, fears, prejudices, needs, desires, and aspirations that, taken together, govern how one behaves," and that in turn, "finds holistic expression in a lifestyle."

RELATING PSYCHOGRAPHICS TO CONSUMER MARKETING.

Psychographics provides the human dimension to understanding consumers and prospects. It is based on the recognition that two individuals may be very much alike demographically, yet act very differently.

Take, for example, two upscale baby boomers: One is wholeheartedly acquisitive while the other purposely disdains whatever is in vogue. It is the psychographic approach that identifies these people's needs, concerns, self-image, and personal style. Responding to the cues that signal how an individual views him/herself can enable the savvy marketer to close the sale more quickly.

With this basic understanding of what demographics and psychographics are, you are ready to explore how changing demographics and psychographics can be used by your business.

Psychographics can be used in two ways:

- To help marketers refine their demographic screening by identifying which groups of individuals (within a pinpointed demographic target) are most likely to buy or not buy a product or service. **This is recommended for low cost, high volume products and services.**

- To help marketers identify the common characteristics of individuals most likely to buy a product or service, which can be used, in turn, to refine the demographic screening. **This is recommended for high cost, smaller volume products and services.**

- **Once we know who, demographically, our target individuals or groups are, we need to understand, psychographically, what makes one individual or group act the same as or differently from another.**

The elements of psychographics are:
  Social Values and Beliefs
  Attitudes, Interests, Opinions
  Lifestyles
  Benefits

INTRODUCING THE VALS DOUBLE TYPOLOGY

While there are numerous psychographic typologies, the best-known is VALS—an acronym for Values and Lifestyles—which grew out of research begun in 1960 at SRI International, a not-for-profit research firm in Menlo Park, California. Its creator, Arnold Mitchell, developed a holistic approach. He drew on insight, and many sources of data, to develop a comprehensive framework for characterizing American ways of life.

The original VALS typology is divided into four major categories, with a total of nine lifestyle types. These lifestyles are fitted together into the VALS double hierarchy. (In mid-1989 SRI announced a new VALS 2 typology, replacing the nine original lifestyle types with eight new psychographic groups. Because—at this date—VALS 2 has not been used extensively, I have chosen to provide the information on VALS 1. All but the most sophisticated of marketers will find it equally pertinent.)

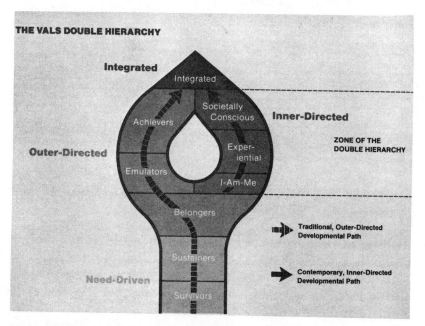

Reprinted with permission of SRI International, Menlo Park, Ca.

THE NINE VALS LIFESTYLES*

■ The **Need-Driven** are people so limited in resources (especially financial resources) that their lives are driven more by need than by choice. Values of the Need-Driven center around survival, safety, and security. Such people tend to be distrustful, dependent, and unplanning. The Need-Driven category can be divided into two lifestyles: *Survivor* and *Sustainer*. Approxi-

---

*This overview of the nine VALS lifestyles is taken from "Styles in the American Bullring" published in *Across the Board*, March 1983.

mately 10 percent of Americans fall into this category, heavily elderly and minority.

> Survivors are the most disadvantaged in American Society by reason of their extreme poverty, low education, old age, and limited access to upward mobility. Many, now infirm, once lived lifestyles associated with higher levels of the VALS hierarchy. Others are ensnared in the "culture of poverty."

> Sustainers are a group struggling at the edge of poverty. They are better off and younger than Survivors, and many have not given up hope. Their values have advanced from depression and hopelessness to expression of anger at the system, and they have developed a street-wise determination to get ahead.

The Need-Driven spend the greatest share of their income on the basics of life: food, shelter, and clothing. They have less disposable income than other VALS groups.

■ The **Outer-Directeds,** comprising between 61 percent and 68 percent of Americans, conduct their lives in response to signals—real or fancied—from others. Consumption, activities, attitudes—all are guided by what the Outer-Directed individual thinks others will think. Psychologically, Outer-Direction is a major step forward from being Need-Driven. Life has broadened to include other people and a host of institutions. In general, the Outer-Directeds are the happiest of Americans, being well-attuned to the cultural mainstream—indeed, creating much of it.

The VALS typology defines three principal types of Outer-Directed people: Belongers, Emulators, and Achievers.

> The Belongers constitute the large, solid, comfortable, middle-class group of Americans who are the main stabilizers of society, and the preservers and defenders of the moral status quo. Belongers tend to be conservative, conventional,

nostalgic, sentimental, puritanical, and con-
forming. The key drive is to fit in—to belong—
and not to stand out. Their road is straight and
narrow, well posted and well lit. Family, church,
and tradition loom large. Belongers are people
who know what is "right," and they adhere to
the rules.

Emulators are trying to break into the upper
levels of the system—to make it big. The object
of their emulation is the *Achiever* lifestyle. In
truth, many are not on the track that will make
them Achievers, but appear not to realize this.
They are ambitious, upwardly mobile, status
conscious, macho, and competitive. Many see
themselves as coming from the wrong side of
the tracks; they are intensely distrustful, and
have little faith that the system will give them a
fair shake.

Psychologically, Emulators are a step ahead of Belongers.
They have assumed greater personal responsibility for getting
ahead, instead of drifting with events in the style of many Belongers. Their emphasis is on acquiring material possessions.
Their psychological stance is "If I can do it, you can do it."

Achievers include many leaders in business, the
professions, and government. Competent, self-
reliant, and efficient, Achievers tend to be mate-
rialistic, hard-working, oriented to fame and
success, and comfort-loving. These are the affluent people who created an economic system
in response to the American dream. As such,
they are the defenders of the economic status
quo. Achievers are among the best adjusted of
Americans, being well-satisfied with their place
in the system.

Hispanic Americans may be the most Outer-Directed of
our four key demographic groups. Although many Hispanic

Americans are currently found in the Needs-Driven categories, large numbers are beginning to find themselves in a better economic position. Because the majority of adult Hispanics are struggling to find a better lifestyle for their families, and are grateful to the United States for making that possible, many will be attracted to the Outer-Directed path at first. Extremely loyal, Hispanic men and women will respond with their trade to those organizations that welcomed them early on.

As Hispanic Americans climb the ladder economically and socially, they will seek out goods and services which show they belong. As do all Outer-Directeds, they will conduct their lives in response to signals, real or fancied, from others. As their lives broaden to include major purchases of automobiles, homes, and luxury items, they will respond to peer pressure and a desire to be part of the "in" group.

■ The **Inner-Directeds** contrast with the Outer-Directeds in that they conduct their lives primarily in accord with inner values—needs and desires private to the individual—rather than in accord with values oriented to externals. Concern with inner growth is a cardinal characteristic.

It is important to recognize that, in American society today, one can hardly be profoundly Inner-Directed without having internalized Outer-Directedness through extensive and deep exposure as a child, adolescent, or adult. One implication is that Inner-Directed people tend not to come from Need-Driven or Inner-Directed families. Some measure of satiation with the pleasures of external things seems to be required before a person can believe in or enjoy the less visible, incorporeal pleasures of Inner-Direction. While the bulk of Americans still cluster around the Outer-Directed pole, the baby boomers have affected the numbers of Inner-Directeds significantly, causing a projected rise in their strength. In 1983, Inner-Directeds were just 19 percent of the American population; today, Inner-Directeds make up 26 percent, with a corresponding decrease to 61 percent in Outer-Directeds.

VALS has identified three stages of Inner-Directedness: I-Am-Me, Experiential, and Societally Conscious.

I-Am-Me is a short-lived stage of transition from Outer- to Inner-Direction. Values from both stages are highly visible. Typically, the I-Am-Me person is young and fiercely individualistic, to the point of being narcissistic and an exhibitionist. People at this stage are full of confusions and emotions they do not understand; they often define themselves better by their actions than by their statements.

I-Am-Me's are a good consumer group to market to, if you can get them to accept you. Computers, leisure and sports, entertainment, clothing, and fast food are all dominated by I-Am-Me's. As the I-Am-Me's mature psychologically, they become the *Experientials*. At this stage of Inner-Direction, the focus has widened from the intense egocentrism of the I-Am-Me to include other people, and many social and human issues. Experientials are people who most want direct experience and vigorous involvement. Life is a light show at one moment and an intense, often mystic, inner experience the next. The most inner-directed of any VALS group, these people are also probably the most articulate and the most passionately involved with others.

Younger women are heavily represented in the Experiential group. Experientials—more than any other VALS group—have short interest-spans and often flit from one cause to another. Experientials tend to enjoy and accept modern gadgetry more than other VALS groups. New technology—such as the FAX—finds its initial acceptance with Experientials. They are also the most physically active VALS group, and strong consumers of leisure and fitness products and services.

The *Societally Conscious* have extended their Inner-Direction beyond the self and others to society as a whole—sometimes to the globe or even, philosophically, to the cosmos. A profound sense of societal responsibility leads these people to support such causes as conservation, environmentalism, and consumerism. They tend to be activistic, impassioned, and knowledgeable about the world around them. Many are attracted to simple living and nature; some have taken up lives of voluntary simplicity.

Most Societally Conscious do not shun possessions. Rather, they look for quality as opposed to quantity. They are selective in their choice of vendors and seek out those organizations which have an identifiable record of accountability. They grow restless with being told about "necessary delivery delays" and can be very innovative in suggesting and accepting different products and services.

■ **Integrateds** are a small group at the pinnacle of the VALS typology. These rare people have put it all together. They meld the power of Outer-Direction with the sensitivity of Inner-Direction. They are fully mature in a psychological sense— able to see many sides of an issue, able to lead if necessary, and willing to take a secondary role if that is appropriate. They usually possess a deep sense of the fittingness of things.

Integrateds possess a deep commitment to making the world a better place for their children and others. They purchase generously, looking for special gifts. Their generosity and vision inspires others. Unfortunately, they exist in extremely small numbers, comprising only 2 to 4 percent of the American population.

The VALS typology is based on theories of psychological development, particularly Abraham Maslow's hierarchy of human needs; so the nine VALS lifestyle categories are seen as more or less stable over time. While these lifestyle categories are not fixed and immutable, movement is commonly no more than a level or two in an individual's lifetime. Many people grow from one level to another from children, to adolescents, to adults. Some very few start at the bottom and reach the top within a lifetime.

Examples of ads that appeal. VALS has been used successfully by businesses and other organizations to target audiences. Chapter 11 presents an example from a builder of single-family homes.

Integrating geo-demographics and psychographics. National Decision Systems and SRI International have devised a way to integrate VISION™ and VALS (see Chapter 2). The forty-eight VISION™ segments have been VALS typed. VISION™ will indicate where these targets live, and link to lifestyles, demographics, and buying behavior.

■ **The VALS methodology.** Surveying constituents for the VALS typology requires using a set of twenty-eight questions available only through SRI or one of its clients. Sample questions might include:

- I like to think I'm a bit of a swinger.

- A communist should not be allowed to run for Mayor in this city.

- It's very important to me to feel I am part of a group.

- My greatest achievements are ahead of me.

- I would rather spend a quiet evening at home than go out to a party.

- I believe a woman can work outside the home, even if she has small children, and still be a good mother.

- Just as the Bible says, the world literally was created in six days.

While a formal VALS methodology may not be feasible for your business—either because using SRI's services is too expensive, or because your organization may be uncomfortable or unable to incorporate sensitive questions such as the examples above into consumer surveys—look for the clues your consumers and potential customers provide as to their psychographics.

■ **Alternative psychographic methodologies are available.** Some methodologies begin by assuming that you have already done the demographic segmentation, and have chosen to concentrate on a particular cohort, for example, baby boomers.

D. *Quinn Mills'* methodology suggests that there are five different groups of boomers:

Competitors	15%
Pleasure Seekers	25%
Trapped	11%
Contented	48%
Get Highs	1%

Mills, a professor at the Harvard Business School, has defined the categories as follows:

- The *competitors* are primarily business-motivated. They are constantly seeking opportunities to advance themselves in their careers. They often get so wrapped up in their work that they can't find time to enjoy life. They are partly motivated by making money. But primarily, they are interested in beating out the other person, in what is a contest to them. They are very interested in new styles or ideas, because they might gain an advantage by being the first to adopt them.

- The *pleasure seekers* are into sports, or activities, or traveling—things other than work. They work primarily to earn enough money to pay for the experiences and things they enjoy. They are spontaneous and generally good-natured. They are not lazy, but devote a lot of time and attention to developing new diversions. They believe the "competitors" are crazy to devote so much energy and effort to work.

- The *trapped* are in situations they can't find a way out of. They are in jobs or situations they hate, or in relationships they wish would end. They sometimes feel they've betrayed their own values; that they've become too much like their parents. They generally are consumed by regret about certain choices they've made that didn't turn out well.

- The *contented* are generally satisfied with their lives. They have achieved acceptance in their communities and experience some enjoyment in their work. They are happy in their relationships. They often avoid setting extreme goals for themselves, in order not to be disappointed and regretful when they fail to achieve them. Often they have been trapped at some stage of their lives—in a bad job or unhappy marriage—but they have always made an effort to get themselves out of a bad situation.

- The *let's get highs* find it difficult to accept the contradictions of everyday life. They are often very sensitive people. But to make themselves feel better, they get high on drugs, alcohol or daredevil adventures. Some take an opposite track and commit themselves wholeheartedly to religions or cults. These are people who go to extremes. Their particular extreme dominates their relationships with other people.

Fred Posner, of N.W. Ayer & Co. Advertising Agency, has suggested using social and behavioral factors to reach baby boomers. He has developed a very simple charting axis. At the top of the axis are people who are extremely innovative. At the bottom of the axis are people who are more traditional. The left side of the axis consists of people who are secure. The right side are people who tend to be more insecure. He has developed four groups based on his tests.

- *Satisfied Selves*, the top left quadrant, are people who are innovative and secure. They comprise 34 percent of boomers, and tend to be the most educated and the wealthiest. This group tends to have the highest percent of two-income households.

- *60s in the 80s*, the extreme upper right-hand quadrant, are people who are innovative but insecure. They tend to be younger boomers and, in a sense, they have never left Woodstock. They are still searching for themselves and are least likely to have children.

- *Contented Traditionalists*, the bottom left quadrant, comprise 31 percent of the boomer population. They are secure Outer-Directeds. Appeal to these boomers in terms of your organization's tradition and history. They correspond to the VALS' "belongers."

- *Worried Traditionalists*, the right bottom quadrant, are less relaxed. They are concerned with security and safety issues.

The Roper Organization has reported on a key consumer group it has dubbed *The Influential Americans*. By definition, they are "the people who play an especially active role in their communities and in the nation." Demographically, they are predominantly in their thirties and forties (baby boomers), are married and have children. They are wealthier than most Americans, and better educated.

In addition to explaining the Influentials' views on politics and public policy, this report tells you how best to reach the Influentials. For businesses concentrating on boomers, "The Roper Report on Influential Americans" provides fascinating insights on the psychographics of this desirable boomer segment:

- **The Personal Values of the Influentials:** the Primacy of the Family, the Role of Religion, the Importance of Work, Education: A Bedrock Value, and Influential Aspirations and Dreams.

- **The Influential Lifestyle:** Social Influentials, Home Entertainment, Health and Fitness Habits, Hobbies and Other Interests, Life's Obligations: What Bores the Influentials, the Need for More Time.

- **The Influentials as Pioneer Consumers:** the Track Record on "New" Products, Loyalties to Specific Brands, the Perceived Credibility of Advertising, Purchase Habits, the Impact of Coupons and Other Promotions, Consumer Dissatisfaction, Influencing Other Consumers.

Understanding psychographics provides you with the ability to refine your target market. Fred Posner may have explained its importance best. N.W. Ayer had asked several hundred ad people to match various companies with the animals that best represented them. "If you're thought of as an ostrich or elephant and you really want to be a tiger or cougar, you'd better change your stripes and start growling," says Posner. Or, you'd better find the consumers who, psychographically, match you better.

CHAPTER FOUR

Demographic, Geo-demographic, and Psychographic Resources

OFTEN, THE BEST SOURCE OF information is the organization that wants to sell you its products and services. Their representatives can provide detailed examples of how businesses, similar to yours, have benefited from their input. Ask for their literature, get on their prospect mailing lists, seek them out at conferences, and/or visit them.

Back in the late 1970s, finding a vendor in the private data field was fairly simple. The second issue of *American Demographics* (February 1979) featured a guide to "The Wonderful World of Private Data Companies"—all twenty-six of them! Now *American Demographics* prints a yearly supplement—highlighting their choice of the best one hundred—to bring timely information to marketers.

The explosion of firms entering the consumer information industry means that any directory is out of date even as it's being printed. By the time you read this chapter, new organizations will be entering the consumer information field and established ones may be leaving. This list draws heavily from *American Demographics'* "The Best 100 Sources for Marketing Information."

A PARTIAL LIST OF RESOURCES FOR DEMOGRAPHIC AND PSYCHOGRAPHIC DATA

GENERAL PUBLICATIONS

American Demographics
P.O. Box 68
Ithaca, NY 14851
800/828-1133

If you only buy one publication, this should be it! Each issue of *American Demographics* provides fascinating articles, examples, and statistics on the impact of demographics and psychographics on the American scene. The magazine always references its sources, so you can go to the organization that compiled the information or conducted the survey if you desire.

The Numbers News
P.O. Box 68
Ithaca, NY 14851
800/828-1133

The Numbers News, a monthly, 12-page newsletter published by American Demographics, Inc., reports the newest facts behind the latest consumer market trends in a quick-read format. Whereas *American Demographics* covers the "big picture," *The Numbers News* concentrates on the numbers behind those consumer trends.

Off the Shelf
2171 Jericho Turnpike
Commack, NY 11725
516/462-2410

Off the Shelf is a bi-monthly free catalog of current market studies, industry and company reports, surveys, and other information publications available from leading U.S. and international publishers.

The Public Pulse
205 East Forty-Second Street
New York, NY 10017
212/599-0700

The Public Pulse, published monthly by The Roper Organization, reports what Americans are thinking, doing, and buying. Issues of the newsletter contain a Research Supplement as well.

Research Alert
37-06 30th Avenue
Long Island City, NY 11103
718/626-3356

Research Alert's bi-monthly issues deliver key findings from ten to twenty new studies, plus detailed listings of an additional twelve to fifteen new consumer reports. A bonus: many of the reports it identifies offer free or inexpensive copies of their research to the public.

The Wall Street Journal
420 Lexington Avenue
New York, NY 10170
212/808-6700

Every business day, *The Wall Street Journal* provides a wealth of information about consumer marketing trends, research, media choices, and other topics of importance to marketers in its ''Marketplace'' section.

Yankelovich MONITOR
8 Wright Street
Westport, CT 06880
203/227-2700

The *Yankelovich MONITOR*, launched in 1970, is the longest standing continuing study of social values, attitudes and behavior.

SPECIALIZED PUBLICATIONS

In addition to *Research Alert* and the *Yankelovich Monitor*, each of which offer specialized newsletters targeting minorities, the affluent, and youth, you can order

The Boomer Report
FIND/SVP, Inc.
625 Avenue of the Americas
New York, NY 10011
212/645-4500

This monthly newsletter monitors the baby boomer generation—what it's buying, thinking, feeling, and doing next.

Marketing to Women
P.O. Box 3434
Boston, MA 02101
617/723-4337

Published monthly, MW covers the latest research on women's demographics, buying habits, attitudes, trends, and lifestyles. It references its sources of information—often available without cost upon request.

DEMOGRAPHIC SERVICES

The organizations listed below are integrators of key information resources for site evaluation, target marketing, market analysis, media selection, and direct marketing. They provide consumer information in several formats.

Donnelley Marketing Information Services
P.O. Box 10250
Stanford, CT 06904
203/353-7474

Impact Resources, Inc.
125 Dillmont Drive
Columbus, OH 43235
614/888-5900

National Demographics & Lifestyles
1621 Eighteenth Street
Denver, CO 80202
800/525-3533

National Decision Systems
Box 9007
Encinitas, CA 92024-9007
619/942-7000

National Planning Data Corporation
P.O. Box 610
Ithaca, NY 14851
607/273-8208

Slater-Hall Information Products
1522 K Street, NW
Washington, DC 20005
202/682-1350

TRW Target Marketing Services
600 City Parkway West, Suite 1000
Orange, CA 92668
714/385-7708

Urban Decision Systems, Inc.
2040 Armacost Avenue
Los Angeles, CA 90025
800/633-9568

GEO-DEMOGRAPHIC SCREENING SERVICES

These organizations provide market analysis and mapping services which integrate your databases with their databases. This process lets you know who your prospects are (and are not) based on the demographic, socioeconomic and housing characteristics of their neighborhoods. PRIZM is Claritas' demographic segmentation system. VISION™ is used by National Decision Systems.

Claritas
201 North Union Street
Alexandria, VA 22314
703/683-8300

National Decision Systems
Box 9007
Encinitas, CA 92024-9007
619/942-7000

PSYCHOGRAPHICS/LIFESTYLES SCREENING SERVICES

These companies provide screening services which link lifestyle information to geo-demographic segmentation. Donnelley Marketing Information Services uses Cluster PLUS; SRI uses VALS.

Donnelley Marketing Information Services
P.O. Box 10250
Stamford, CT 06904
203/353-7207

SRI International
333 Ravenswood Avenue
Menlo Park, CA 94025
415/859-3882

PART II

BUILDING YOUR CONSUMER BASE
IN THE 1990s

Martha Farnsworth Riche, editor of *The Numbers News*—a prize-winning newsletter that covers all aspects of demographic data—and a senior editor of *American Demographics*, says that the world exists as measured in terms of "bodies and bucks."

To me, that seems a fair summary of what marketing is all about: finding the people who will spend the dollars. Marketers have a dual need: **short-term,** to cultivate and solicit the current pool of prospects for maximum purchasing, and **long-term,** to prepare for the future by being alert to opportunities to expand and upgrade the consumer base. Selling and prospecting must be done concurrently. Doing both jobs successfully requires understanding who are our current consumers, as well as identifying who our prospects are likely to be.

For marketers, the 1990s already look very different from the 1980s. Riche suggests* that the emphasis is shifting from "exploring new markets to exploiting existing ones."

In other words, the pool of potential customers/consumers is not unlimited. Recognizing that your organization has competition—locally, regionally, nationally, even globally—means that you need to use information to make your existing markets more profitable.

Riche used the example of the John Hancock Insurance Company, which segments its customers by demographics, psychographics, and recent life events, such as births and marriages. That enables the company to zero in on two targets: small segments that buy a lot of insurance, and larger segments that buy enough insurance to create economies of scale.

To succeed in the 1990s, Riche suggests, your organization must "produce a holistic marketing program, one that respects the identity of each customer segment while recognizing its contribution to a profitable whole."

---

*January 1990 issue of American Demographics.

CHAPTER FIVE

Targeting Baby Boomers

BECAUSE OF THEIR SHEER num-
bers, baby boomers are a necessary marketing target for every
business. The boomer generation is one-third of America; one-
half of all adults. Because boomers are just gaining the economic and political power to shape events, they will be even
more important to your business in the years ahead.

WHO ARE THE BABY BOOMERS?

■ **Boomers are the "Mouse in the Snake."** Seventy-six million
people were born between 1946 and 1964. Their impact on our
society, at every stage of their lives, has often been compared to
the results of a very large mouse going through a very small
snake.

In the early 1950s, boomers created growth industries of
baby furniture, diaper delivery services, and toy companies.
Gerber boasted that "babies are our business—our only business." In the late 1950s, fads like hoola hoops and raccoon caps
swept the nation. In the 1960s, rock music, fast food and
snacks, and acne coverups were the rage; then psychedelic
fashions, art, and expressions took hold. The 1970s? Boomers
settling down caused housing costs to skyrocket.

Today, as boomers swell the ranks of those age 35 to 44,
they are redefining the idea of middle-age. Having elevated fitness to a cult, baby boomers are now putting the stamp of ap-

BABY BOOM POPULATION

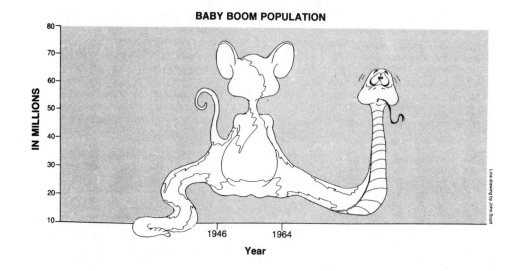

Reprinted from "Targeting Baby Boomers For Fund Raising," Judith E. Nichols, permission of *Fund Raising Management*, May 1989.

proval on plastic surgery. Having discoed their early adult lives away, boomers are becoming couch potatoes, and cocooning. Having defined a "youth market" for soft drinks and facial cleaning products, boomers are now Madison Avenue's targets for Geritol and Oil of Olay.

■ **A Generation of Emerging Economic Power.** With maturity, baby boomers are entering their peak earning years. "The generation is just gaining the economic and political power to shape events," says Bickley Townsend, vice president of The Roper Organization, and a contributing editor of *American Demographics*. "The sheer numbers, and their power, mean they will determine which businesses succeed and which fail. Whatever the Baby Boom wants, the Baby Boom is going to get."

Many boomers feel it's about time. Although boomers are better educated (twice as likely to have gone to college as their parents), their sheer numbers, coupled with a series of rude social and economic shocks (ranging from the Vietnam War to double-digit inflation), have depressed their disposable incomes. Boomers marry later, have children later, and divorce more often. *Time* magazine, quoting boomer Brian Weiss in a cover story, "Growing Pains at 40," notes that for many boomers, "Middle age sounds a bit strange because many of us haven't attained the goals that our parents attained at that age. I mean, how can you be an adult when you don't own a house?"

Landon Y. Jones* agrees, but sounds a note of hope.

> Oppressed by its numbers, the boom generation watched its great expectations yield to diminishing expectations as its troubles piled up. By the end of the seventies, *Fortune Magazine* estimated, the baby boomers had effectively lost ten years' income relative to the cohort just ahead of them and hardly seemed to have reason to look forward to the future. But that's not the case. In the next decade the baby boom will be moving into its Golden Era. The smoking friction associated with its size will, for once, be minimized.
>
> During the 1990s, baby boomers will move into their prime earning years, causing the number of affluent households to inflate to unprecedented heights. Increasing numbers of baby boomers will turn their education, job experience, marital stability, and investments into a secure income. The number of householders aged 35 to 54 will swell by 40 percent, from 31 million in 1986 to 44 million by 2000. Those with the highest annual incomes—$75,000 and over—will increase from 2.2 million to 6.2 million, accounting for one in seven households in this age group by the turn of the century.

■ **Segmenting boomers demographically.** The size of the boomer cohort is so large that to market effectively we need to define submarkets:

Using education and income, Peter Kim, senior vice president at the J. Walter Thompson Company, suggests a four-cell demographic segmentation.

---

*His landmark biography of the baby boom, *Great Expectations*, chronicles the most-recorded generation in America's history.

Boomer Submarkets

- **Superclass** (Yuppies): high education/high income
  with personal incomes of $51,000—6% of boomers

- **Elite Workers:** low education/high income
  with personal incomes of $45,000—4.4% of boomers

- **Would-Be's:** high education/low income
  with personal incomes of $18,000—22% of boomers

- **Workers:** low education/low income
  with personal incomes of $14,000—67% of boomers

Many marketers will target the emerging **Superclass** of boomers, especially for upscale or high-ticket purchases. Kim projects that with the growth of affluence, by 1995 11 percent of baby boomers will belong to the Superclass.

> "They are most visible on the two coasts," notes Landon Jones. "In New York and Boston and in San Francisco and Los Angeles—and their capital is Washington, D.C. They are growing in power because they are socioeconomically distinct from most other Americans. They are the professional-managerial working couples who command more discretionary income than any other group. They dress differently from most people, entertain themselves differently, eat differently, travel to different places, buy different things, and have different values. They have far fewer children."

But the Superclass is only a small part of the overall boomer generation. You should cultivate **Elite Workers** as well. By 1995, they will double in number to 9 percent.

Would-Be's will then account for 18 percent of baby boomers, and **Workers** for 63 percent. Should we ignore Would-Be's and Workers? Probably not. If your product or service appeals to either or both of these boomer sub-segments, the sheer numbers make them worth pursuing.

And, while these boomers—as individuals—may not

Households Headed by Persons Aged 35 to 54, by Income: 1986-2000

	1986	1990	1995	2000
All households	31,099	34,269	39,707	43,665
Under $10,000.	3,557	3,660	3,963	4,074
$10,000 to $19,999.	4,943	5,046	5,418	5,521
$20,000 to $29,999	5,889	6,007	6,434	6,534
$30,000 to $39,999	5,494	5,845	6,488	6,781
$40,000 to $49,999	3,982	4,608	5,460	6,006
$50,000 to $59,999	2,803	3,148	3,782	4,331
$60,000 to $74,999.	2,165	2,767	3,545	4,214
$75,000 and over. . .	2,266	3,186	4,618	6,205
Median income. . . .	$32,110	$34,140	$36,230	$38,410

(households in thousands; income is for previous year and is in 1985 dollars)

Source: *American Demographics*, November 1987.

have the income demographics you may seek, as *couples* they are often doing very nicely. **Remember that, whether in a formal marriage or more informal living arrangement, the majority of boomer households contains two full-time working adults.** In fact, by the year 2000, nearly 15 million households headed by 35- to 54-year-olds will have incomes of $50,000 or more (in current dollars).

■ **Psychographically, boomers are both similar to and distinctly different from other generations:** *"In many ways, boomers' primary concerns are the same as their parents and grandparents: home, marriage, family, and work,"* according to Cheryl Russell.* Boomers are:

---

*Editor-in-chief of *American Demographics* and author of *100 Predictions for the Baby Boom*.

- married, and they believe that marriage is the best way to live

- have one or two children, and many have three

- prefer to spend their free time at home with their families

- have middle-class incomes and are unwilling to take financial risks

- identify themselves politically as middle-of-the-road or conservative

- favor capital punishment

- believe in God and belong to a church

But, notes Russell, "in many ways the baby boom is profoundly different from any generation in history. This means that in the two decades of middle-aged rule that lie ahead, many of the themes important to successful marketing will be new ones. **There are four important new themes: globalism, unisex, individualism, and instant gratification.**" Russell cautions that if you dig a little deeper, you will find that boomers:

- have gone to college for at least one year and many are college graduates

- are two-income couples

- believe men and women should be equally responsible for housecleaning

- own VCRs and microwaves; many have home computers and telephone answering machines

- think imports are better than American-made products

- frequently go to movies, plays, concerts, and museums

- think divorce is acceptable and abortion should be legal

D. Quinn Mills, a professor at the Harvard Business School who teaches courses in human resource management, concurs that "the basic values and aspirations of the baby boom generation differ substantially from those of their parents." Contrasted with their parents, boomers:

- are more suspicious of authority (though leadership is accepted by both generations)

- stress fun and enjoyment rather than duty and obligation

- emphasize performance rather than time in grade and experience

- focus on opportunity rather than security

- endorse candor rather than tact

- are self-concerned rather than organization-loyal

- stress individuality and differences rather than groups and sameness

- prefer experience to possessions

As we move through the 1990s and into the twenty-first century, the graying of the baby boom will redefine aging. Between 1990 and 2000, the age 45 to 54 population segment alone will grow by 45 percent. Because boomers are a unique combination of traditional and nontraditional values, it's being suggested that the 1990s will resemble the 1950s, but will be less conventional.

> **"The trick in marketing to the new middle-aged is that you will have to bridge the similarities and differences between the baby boom and older generations of Americans,"** concludes Russell. "If you pursue only the similarities, you might attract older Americans—those 50 and older—to whatever you're selling, but you won't attract the bulk of baby boomers. If you pursue only the differences, you might appeal to the minority of baby boomers who are single and childless, but you'll miss most of the boom generation."

■ **Smart marketers will also segment early boomers from later boomers.** Those who were born in the beginning years of the baby boom—from 1946 to 1956—differ psychographically from those who followed in the years 1956 to 1962.

Early boomers found the going rougher than did later boomers. They were rudely confronted with the reality of intense competition from their peers. Later boomers are less idealistic and more realistic than their earlier cohorts. While early boomers majored in philosophy and the arts, later boomers opted for business and engineering.

One late boomer noted that "it's like, we don't even have a name. Yours—'baby boomers'—is so big we fall in its shadow. We're hard to pin down: silent where you were loud, solitary where you were communal, plain where you were colorful."

FORECASTING BOOMER-DRIVEN NICHES AND NEEDS

When one-half your adult population fits a demographic segmentation, they will be the primary target for the majority of businesses. Thus it is with the baby boomers.

There are three key factors to keep in mind when looking for boomer-driven niches and needs:

■ **Boomers are an aging population.** Currently in or approaching their forties, boomers are giving new meaning to "middle age." As the "mouse in the snake," boomers will redefine every step of their aging.

■ **Boomers are a "held-back" cohort.** They marry later, divorce more often, have children later, and often have split families. They're fueling a baby boomlet which will send ripples through those products and services targeted to families and youth.

■ **Boomers are a "sandwiched" generation.** Often boomers—especially boomer women—are dealing with the concerns and needs of aging parents and grandparents, as well as the needs of their growing families.

The five broad categories for which demographers and forecasters foresee significant growth in the 1990s are highlighted in Part 3. Baby boomers will play a key role in fueling increased demand for products and services for the home, education, health and fitness, leisure time, and financial planning.

MARKETING KEYS FOR BABY BOOMERS

Although baby boomers are diverse both demographically and psychographically, there are many shared characteristics that you can use in your marketing.

■ **Recognize that boomers appear to have less "brand" loyalty, generally, than other Americans.** Businesses may find themselves benefiting and losing boomers as consumers according to fleeting interest(s). A full discussion of this aspect can be found in Chapter 16.

Treat boomers as individuals. Baby boomers are fond of discovering products and places that have been overlooked, possibly because of their sense of constant competition. This may bode well for smaller businesses, and those larger organizations that personalize their approach.

Accountability is important to boomers. Keep costs reasonable, and explain price increases in a way that can be understood and documented.

Straight talk and honest emotion appeal to boomers, says John Gorman, founder of Epsilon Data Management, a database marketer based in Burlington, Massachusetts. "People don't relate to generalities or talk-down-to-them copy," he says. "They have to be approached conversationally and told about real programs, case histories, and successes."

Use appeals that grab their attention. The boomer generation is a stimuli-bombarded generation. As Cheryl Russell notes, the power of instant communication has magnified the baby boom's size. "Not only does the baby boom have a loud voice, it has a loudspeaker wired into every home." Ads should be fast-moving, with quick cut-aways and facial close-ups to create visual excitement. Use short paragraphs, colorful envelopes, and catchy headlines that a boomer can read quickly at the end of a busy day.

■ **Boomers thrive on professional and personal networking opportunities.** They mix work and pleasure. Innovation is the key to attracting their attention. Marketing themes that focus on nostalgia for the 1950s and early 1960s (music, dress, trivia) are well received.

■ **Concentrate on consumer recognition.** Because many boomers like immediate gratification, don't let too much time go by between the sale and an acknowledgment. Consider forming some kind of "club" for your customers. Membership cards, signalling being a part of the "in" group, and invitations to VIP or pre-general public events, available to members only, contribute to the boomer's sense of elitism through participation.

■ **Allow time for decision-making.** Direct response marketing—direct mail, point of purchase, and telemarketing—may need to be modified because they send the wrong messages to boomer audiences. As a group, boomers have significantly more education than previous generations. They want to be treated as professionals, and will identify themselves as a "professional bus driver," "professional welder," or "professional bartender," according to D. Quinn Mills.

■ **Focus on instant gratification.** Use credit card payments and monthly payment plans to encourage boomers to make larger purchases using smaller payments. Most boomers have grown up on "buy now, pay later." Payments that start one, three, and six months after the purchase are very popular with boomers.

■ **Communicate clearly, sharply, and visually.** Don't be afraid to use new technologies such as FAX, VCRs, and computers to personalize your message, and make it stand out from the messages of other organizations. Baby boomers enjoy receiving information, but are quick to become impatient with boring formats.

■ **Use nostalgia.** "Nostalgia waxes and wanes, and it's certainly waxing now, as the baby boom generation passes into phases of life that create conditions that can elicit nostalgic responses," says Fred Davis.* He and other academics say marriage, parenthood and the leveling off of careers in the late 30s and 40s are typically followed by an unsettled period in people's lives, when they look back to childhood for comfort.

Reaching back to boomers' adolescent years—especially pre-1963, which many boomers associate as the start of the "bad times"—for marketing creates instant identification. Many of the old slogans, "I want my Maypo," "Takes a licking but keeps on ticking," "M'm! M'm! Good!" are being brought back; other businesses are using music, television, and film to recreate memories.

> The familiar faces of two TV moms are drawing attention to a new TV commercial for an otherwise dull product.
> Starring in the ad: Barbara Billingsley—June Cleaver on "Leave It to Beaver," and Jane Wyatt—Margaret Anderson on "Father Knows Best." They drink tea and chat, in a very low-key way, about Philips' Milk of Magnesia laxative.
> "We're here to gently remind you....," says Wyatt. Billingsley finishes the sentence, "...that

---

*A professor at the University of California at San Diego, and the author of *Yearning for Yesterday: A Sociology of Nostalgia.*

you can depend on your M.O.M.'' That's an acronym created by N.W. Ayer Inc., the agency handling the Milk of Magnesia account, to help you remember the product name.

After an announcer reads the slogan: ''Nobody treats you better than M.O.M.''—the two video parents return. ''M.O.M. knows best,'' smiles Wyatt. ''Leave it to M.O.M.,'' laughs Billingsley.

Source: USA TODAY "Moms pitch M.O.M."

■ **Cultivate boomers now for the future.** Because boomers are marrying and having children later—or with divorce, repeating their families—many are still caught in high expenditure years. With the emptying of the nests and their increasing economic assimilation, boomers will be the audience of the future for almost all products and services.

Perhaps most importantly, remember that most boomers are *not* yuppies. Although the media has zeroed in on the stereotype of the ''ultimate consumer,'' most boomers do not fit neatly into any one category. Some are middle-American Outer-Directeds; some have not out-grown the sixties. It's dangerous to generalize too much. Use psychographic tools to put the ''flesh'' on your boomer prospects.

CHAPTER SIX

Targeting the Hispanic Majority

"*F*ORGET SENIORS. FORGET yuppies. Forget female professionals. For sheer numbers and purchasing power, it is immigrants, most of them now from Asia and Latin America, who represent the fastest-growing domestic markets." That's the advice of Joel Kotkin, writing in *Inc.* magazine.

HISPANICS: THE EMERGING MAJORITY

Today, minorities of all ages constitute 20 to 25 percent of our total population in the United States. By the year 2000, one out of every three Americans will be nonwhite. The 1980 census shows that the average white American is 31 years old, the average black American is 26, and the average Hispanic American is just 22.

Hispanic Growth, 1980–2000
Population in millions

```
30 . . . . . . . . . . . . . . . . . . . . . . . . . . . . . .  22.2 . . . . . . .
20 . . . . . . . . . . . . . . . . . . . . . . 16.8 . . . . . . . . . . . . . . . .
10 . . . . . . . . . . . 12.0 . . . . . . . . . . . . . . . . . . . . . . . . . . .
 0

          1980              1990              2000
```

When demographers look to the future, they see Hispanic Americans as the emerging majority in the United States. Currently, the Hispanic population is 18.8 million, or 7.5 percent of the total U.S. population. It has increased 30 percent, nearly one-third, since 1980; the non-Hispanic population has increased only 5.8 percent. Hispanics are increasing about 3.3 percent per year, or about three times the overall U.S. growth rate. **At the present rate of increase, Hispanics, by 1997, will account for one in 10 Americans.**

It is estimated that only thirty years from now, Hispanics will surpass blacks as the largest minority group in the United States. By the year 2020, there will be 47,000,000 Hispanics in the U.S., and within a century, Hispanics could comprise up to 30 percent of the U.S. population, approximately 99,000,000 people.

ECONOMIC IMPLICATIONS

It makes good sense to cultivate the emerging Hispanic majority. Not only are the numbers growing, but economically, Hispanic Americans are gaining. Each year since 1982, the Census Bureau has compiled a report on the Hispanic population of the United States. The 1988 edition indicates two significant trends: the rising Hispanic education level, and the growing number of Hispanic workers in professional and managerial jobs. And, contrary to the stereotypes, most Hispanics are not poor. In 1988, their median family income was $21,800, versus $32,000 for all families.

From 1984 to 1988, the number of Hispanics completing high school increased 34 percent, and the number of Hispanics with four or more years of college jumped 51 percent. During the same time, the number of Hispanic men in the labor force increased 22 percent, while the number of Hispanic men in managerial and professional jobs increased 42 percent. This trend is even stronger for Hispanic women. From 1984 to 1988, the number of Hispanic women in the labor force grew by 24 percent, while the number of Hispanic women working as managers and professionals jumped 61 percent.

As a result of these gains, the share of Hispanic families with annual incomes of at least $25,000 increased for the sixth consecutive year, reaching 41 percent in 1987.

California, always a trend leader, began acknowledging the economic power of its Hispanic population in late 1988. *Los Angeles Magazine* profiled the "Brown Elite"—Mexican Americans who have made it big. The *Los Angeles Times Magazine* featured an article entitled "New Prosperity, New Power," which told "tales of the Emerging Elite."

WHO ARE HISPANIC AMERICANS?

Hispanic is an ethnic category. Half of our Hispanics live in California and Texas; if New York and Florida are added, those four states contain more than two of every three Hispanics living in the United States. However, being Hispanic means different things depending on where you live. In New York, the dominant Hispanic group is Puerto Rican; in Texas, California and other parts of the Southwest, it's Mexican; in Florida, it's Cuban. There are also Hispanics from the Dominican Republic, Columbia and other Latin American countries, and Spain.

■ **There are significant demographic differences between Hispanic groupings.** The Ford Foundation notes that "Today, the U.S. Hispanic population is young, growing, and highly urbanized. It is multiracial, containing blacks, browns, and whites. Its attachment to the Spanish language and Hispanic culture is strong. Far from being monolithic, it is composed of distinct Spanish-origin groups, each of them concentrated in a different region of the country. While tied together by a common cultural background, language, and religion, these groups present distinct social and economic profiles. In the years ahead, they will have an increasing impact on many cities and states—on their politics, their public services, and their social and civic life."

● **Mexican Hispanics** are the youngest Hispanic ethnic group, with a median age of 23, compared to the white American median age of 30. More than one-third are younger than 15, and only 3 percent are over 65 years of age. The 12.1 million Americans of Mexican origin account for 63 percent of all Hispanics. Between 1980 and 1987, Hispanics of Mexican origin grew by 40 percent. While the median family income of other

Hispanic groups has been growing, the median family income of Mexican Americans fell by 6 percent, perhaps because illegals—many of them earning poverty-level wages—are driving much of the growth in the Mexican American population. In 1987, their median income was $20,200.

● **Americans of Puerto Rican origin** account for 12 percent (2.5 million) of Hispanics. Puerto Ricans have a median age of 24 but nearly one-third are younger. Although their birth rate is high, it is lower than that of Mexican Americans. Because of these different growth rates, the Puerto Rican share of the Hispanic population has declined slightly since 1980, even though they have increased by 25 percent. Puerto Ricans also lag behind in income with a median family income of just $15,200. Nearly one in four of the Puerto Rican women who gave birth in 1979 were teenagers. One-third of Puerto Rican families are headed by women alone.

● **Cuban Americans'** demographic profile is markedly different. The median age of Miami's Cubans is 41. Only 15 percent are under 15. Almost 15 percent are over 65 years of age. Cuban Americans are the most affluent Hispanics, with an average family income in 1987 of $27,300. Cubans account for 5 percent (1 million) of Hispanics—the smallest Hispanic ethnic group.

Cuban Hispanics have had a head start on other Hispanic ethnic groups. Many Cubans who immigrated to the U.S. in the 1960s were middle-class, educated people who brought money and skills. Seventeen percent of Cuban Americans age 25 and older have completed four or more years of college. And, partly because a larger proportion of Cuban families are married couples, there are two or more earners in 58 percent of Cuban families.

● **Central and South Americans** account for 11 percent (2.1 million) of the Hispanic population; those of Spanish or "other" origins account for 8 percent (1.6 million). This is the fastest-growing grouping of Hispanics, rising 40 percent between 1981 and 1987. Because of this, the ethnic composition of the Hispanic population is changing. Immigrants from the

Dominican Republic, for example, will surpass Puerto Ricans to become the largest group of foreign-born New York City residents by 1990. Dominicans tend to have a higher socioeconomic status than Puerto Ricans, and consider themselves a separate Hispanic group.

Central and South Americans rank second with $22,900. They have a median age of 27.3 years. "Other" Hispanics are the second oldest ethnic group, with a median age of 30.9 years; they have the third highest median family income, at $21,200.

SHOULD YOUR BUSINESS CONCENTRATE ON ATTRACTING HISPANIC AMERICANS?

According to Alaniz & Sons' (Mt. Pleasant, Iowa) Hispanic Direct division, **the top ten Hispanic markets are:**

1. **Los Angeles:** Seven county area boasting 3,614,000 Hispanics. 70% Mexican, 14% Salvadoran, 7% Guatemalan, 5% Cuban. Seven out of ten speak Spanish at home. Thirty percent of heads-of-household are white-collar workers, 22% are blue-collar, 29% are laborers.

2. **New York:** Four state area (NY, NJ, PA, CT) comprising 2,495,000 persons. Fifty-eight percent Puerto Rican, 26% Dominican, 14% Central and South American. Seven out of ten speak Spanish as their preferred at-home language.

3. **Miami:** Three county area, population of 936,200 Hispanics, 80% Cuban. Nine out of ten use Spanish at home. Thirty percent of heads-of-household are white-collar professionals, 50% are blue-collar workers, 20% are retired, students or unemployed.

4. **San Antonio:** Twenty-eight county ADI (area of dominant influence) with a population of 889,000 persons of Hispanic background. Over 90% Mexican. Spanish is the preferred at-home language of 44%. Twelve percent of heads-of-household are white-collar professionals, 56% hold blue-collar jobs.

5. **San Francisco:** Eleven county ADI, comprising 796,900 Hispanics. Fifty percent Mexican, 15% Salvadoran, 7% Nicaraguan, 4% Argentines and Guatemalans. Sixty-four percent prefer Spanish as the at-home language.

6. **Chicago:** Two state ADI (IL, IN) with 753,700 Hispanics. Cross-sectionally, most representative of U.S. Hispanic population. Sixty-three percent Mexican, 21% Puerto Rican, 3% Cuban, 12% Central and South American. Seven out of ten speak Spanish at home.

7. **Houston:** Twenty county ADI with 706,500 Hispanics, 90% Mexican. Two-thirds use Spanish at home. Twenty-five percent of heads-of-household are white-collar workers, over 50% are blue collar.

8. **McAllen/Brownsville:** Four county area with a population of 588,300 Hispanics. Over ninety percent Mexican. Half speak Spanish at home.

9. **El Paso:** Two state ADI—New Mexico and Texas (does not include sister city of Juarez, Mexico) with 477,900 Hispanics. Ninety-five percent are Mexicans. Six out of ten speak Spanish in the home.

10. **Albuquerque:** Three state ADI (AZ, CO, NM) with a Hispanic population of 451,300. The 1980 census showed that 39% were Mexican, and 41% were other Hispanic. Language preference falls roughly in thirds: Spanish, English, and bilingual.

■ **If you are located in one of the ten Hispanic American growth areas, you should be marketing to Hispanic Americans now.** If your products and services appeal primarily to youth—or to the parents, family and friends of youth—your future target will be Hispanic Americans as well.

MARKETING TO HISPANIC DIVERSITY

There is no mass Hispanic market, just as, in reality, there is little mass baby boomer market. However, you can use *the* many shared characteristics—respect for the past on both personal and historical levels; a highly developed sense of community; a shared language; and a strong sense of family—to guide you if you are serious about attracting Hispanic American consumers.

The Pocket Book of Hispanic Facts, published by Alaniz & Sons, is an excellent resource for marketers. It reminds us that the buying power of the Hispanic market is $160 billion and gaining. Hispanic Facts offers these points to consider:

- Hispanics tend to be Spanish-speaking.

- Between 80 and 90 percent of Hispanics are Roman Catholic.

- Hispanics are extremely brand loyal.

- They are Outer-Directed, and spend more on national brands and popular brands than the general population.

- They are very family oriented.

- Hispanics put great emphasis on the importance of higher education.

- The family and the community comes first.

- Major purchasing decisions tend to be made by the man of the household.

- There is strong geographic clustering.

■ **You may need to place your marketing emphasis on attracting Hispanic Americans as first time consumers.** Remember: Hispanics are loyal, extremely loyal, to the person and/or organization who does right by them. They will deal with you again and again. Once you have attracted a Hispanic customer to your product or service, renewal efforts can be most rewarding. The difficulty is in acquiring the Hispanic consumer.

Encouraging Hispanic consumers requires special efforts that take into account cultural differences. Businesses must be sensitive to the different economic and educational backgrounds of Hispanics coming into the United States.

■ **Hispanic-Americans are more likely than non-Hispanics to rate national and popular brands as being superior to store or local brands.** If yours is a product or a franchise with a strong national reputation and a history going back many years, emphasize this in your promotional material. And, if you can attract the support of a popular spokesperson, use testimonials.

■ **Seven out of ten Hispanics nationwide view themselves as Hispanic first and American second.** Over 66 percent of U.S. Hispanics speak Spanish as their preferred at-home language. Make sure that your communication vehicles are inclusive of Hispanics: Use photographs that demonstrate they are part of your organization's "family." Consider offering readers a choice of language—automatically sending literature written in Spanish can backfire. Many younger Hispanics pride themselves on their English-language skills and will take offense at receiving unrequested Spanish materials.

Retail businesses and those who take phone orders should have staff, *readily available,* who are bilingual. Again, do not assume your Hispanic customer wants to use Spanish, but make sure you are prepared to respond if he/she is more comfortable in Spanish than English.

■ **Hispanics respond most highly of all groups to direct mail coupons.** A survey by Donnelley Marketing finds that approximately 88 percent of Hispanic households redeem coupons, compared to 77 percent for the U.S. average. Response vehicles aimed at Hispanic audiences should always include a coupon. (This is a good place to ask if the prospect would like future materials sent in English or Spanish.)

■ **Co-sponsor community oriented events.** Be a part of the community by underwriting the cost of its festivals and celebrations. Festivals, fairs, and other community events draw large crowds in the Hispanic community, and provide an ideal opportunity to build awareness for your business. Major corporations like Pepsi-Cola, Coca-Cola, Metropolitan Life, and the Adolph Coors Company have already discovered the most effective way to market to Hispanics: link advertising to strong in-community promotional efforts. Chapter 18 provides examples of using community/corporate partnerships.

■ **Hispanics are more family-oriented than non-Hispanics.** Eighty-seven percent reside in households with their families, versus 69 percent of the rest of the U.S. population. Decisions about major purchases tend to be made by the man of the house, but "family input" is very important. Offer in-store events that welcome the entire family. In your ads, use photographs that show multi-generational and extended families.

■ **Incorporate Hispanic themes into your marketing efforts.** There is a wealth of culture and heritage—traditions, food, games, music, art—that can be incorporated into your organization's events and literature. It will convey a message: We welcome Hispanic American participation.

Time magazine saluted the influence of Hispanics with a cover section, "A Latin Wave Hits the Mainstream." Waxing poetic, Time noted:

> Nowadays the mainstream is receiving a rich new current. More and more, American film, theater, music, design, dance and art are taking on a Hispanic color and spirit. Look around. You can see the special lightning, the distinctive gravity, the portable wit, the personal spin.... With each fresh connection tastes are being rebuilt, new understandings concluded. The American mind is adding a new wing.

■ **Hispanic-Americans respond to brighter colors and bolder graphics than do non-Hispanics.** Look at your store's decor and at communication vehicles from your Hispanic customer's point of view. Pale pastels and ornate typestyles are not inviting to these consumers.

- **Market to the Hispanic families who own VCRs;** more than half of the population. If your product or service lends itself to an educational tape, offer it in both English and Spanish versions (prospect's choice). Market the tapes through direct mail with response coupons.

The key to marketing to minorities is to treat them with respect for their own cultures and traditions, while providing tools and opportunities to break down barriers. Hispanic Americans need to feel their patronage is genuinely welcome and valued.

CHAPTER SEVEN

Targeting Aging America

IF YOU HAVEN'T NOTICED, **America is turning gray.** During the past two decades, the number of persons age 45 or older grew almost 30 percent more than the rest of the population.

THE "AGE WAVE" IS COMING

America will never again be a society of youth. Not only are people living longer, but the demographics of the aging baby boomer "hump," plus the lowering of the birth rate, guarantees that older Americans will, increasingly, be the focus of our society. Ken Dychtwald calls this **Age Wave** the "most important trend of our time." In his book of the same name, Dychtwald says that three separate and unprecedented demographic phenomena are converging to produce the coming Age Wave:

■ **The senior boom:** Americans are living longer than ever before, and older Americans are healthier, more active, more vigorous, and more influential than any other older generation in history.

  "Since this century began," says Robert B. Maxwell, vice president of the American Association of Retired Persons, "there has been a 26-year gain in average life expectancy. That nearly equals the gain attained in the previous 5,000 years of human history."

■ **The birth dearth:** A decade ago, fertility in the United States plummeted to its lowest point ever. It has been hovering there ever since, and it's not likely to change. The great population of elders is not being offset by an explosion of children.

■ **The aging of the baby boomer:** The leading edge of the boomer generation has now passed 40. As the boomers approach 50 and pass it, their numbers will combine with the other two great demographic changes to produce a historic shift in the concerns, structure, and style of America.

> Consider these facts:
>
> • In 1991, the first of 76 million baby boomers will join the 45-plus group.
>
> • Between 1990 and 2000, the age 45 to 54 segment alone will increase by 46 percent, versus overall population growth of only 7 percent.
>
> • By 2000, over 61 million adults will be in the "Prime life" generation (age 45 to 64)—nearly as many individuals as there are in the *entire* 50-plus market today.

Nearly one-third of Americans are either in the "prime life" (45-64) or "senior" (65-plus) groups. Together, they represent close to half the entire adult market.*

In 1983, more people were over 65 in America than were teenagers. Because of the baby boomers, that condition will continue. **Every day 5,000 people turn 65 years of age.** The number of older Americans continues to grow dramatically. About 210 Americans become 100 years old every week; as of 1980, the United States had 30,000 people over 100 and 2.2 million over 85.

The over-50 population is growing steadily, while the

---

*According to Jeff Ostroff, author of *Successful Marketing to the 50-Plus Consumer*, and vice president of the PrimeLife Marketing Division of The Data Group, Inc. (Plymouth Meeting, Pa.).

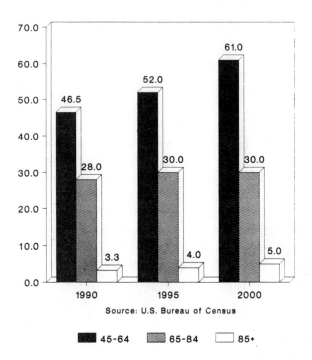

PRIME LIFE (45-64)/SENIOR (65+) CONSUMERS
1990-2000 (in millions)

Source: U.S. Bureau of Census

■ 45-64   ▨ 65-84   ☐ 85+

Reprinted from "Outstanding Business Opportunities in a Graying America" with permission of Prime Life Marketing℠ Division of The Data Group, Inc.

numbers among younger generations are lagging. The average age of Americans is climbing; it is currently 32.5 years. By the year 2000, 28 percent of the total population will be over age 50. Add in baby boomers, who will come of age in the early 2000s, and older people will attain near-majority status in the next several decades. You need to cultivate the "older" (age 50 to 64) and aging boomer populations for the years ahead. Recognize that the number of people age 50 to 64 will start to grow rapidly beginning in the 1990s. By 2020, there will be 81 percent more people in this age group than there are today.

Although they represent only 25 percent of the total U.S. population, Americans over 50 have a combined annual personal income of over $800 billion. They control 70 percent of the total net worth of U.S. households—nearly $7 trillion of wealth.

THIS IS THE LONGEVITY REVOLUTION

Landon Jones, in *Great Expectations*, calls the aging of America "a population revolution that can be compared to the other great upheavals of the American social order; the opening of the frontier, the Industrial Revolution, the wave of European immigration after the Civil War, and the internal migration from the farms to the cities. When this century began, there were perhaps 3 million people in this country over 65, or about 4 percent of the population. When the century closes, there will be 31 million people over 65, comprising more than 12 percent of the population. And before the baby boom is finished, there will be 55 million people over 65 and they will amount to 18 percent of the population."

Population 65 and Over

Year	Number (millions)	Percent Change	Percent of Population	Median Age
1980	24.9	—	11.2	30.2
1990	29.8	+ 20	12.2	32.8
2000	31.8	+ 7	12.2	35.5
2010	34.8	+ 9	12.7	36.6
2020	45.1	+ 30	15.5	37.0
2030	55.0	+ 22	18.3	38.0
2040	54.9	- 1	17.8	37.8

Source: U.S. Bureau of the Census, "Estimates of the Population: 1977-2050" from *Great Expectations*, Landon Jones, pg 369.

Another way of viewing the dramatic increase in lifespan is to put it into historical perspective:

1000 AD	—	life expectancy was 25 years
1700 AD	—	life expectancy was 35 years
1900 AD	—	life expectancy was 45 years
1980 AD	—	life expectancy was 75 years
1990 AD	—	life expectancy is 93 years

It's no wonder that Hallmark Greeting Cards now offers a line of birthday cards hailing the 100th year milestone!

Today's mature market is more properly viewed as having four distinct demographic sub-groups:

■ **The "older" population (age 50 to 64):** Totalling 33 million in 1987. This is the largest segment of the mature market. This group will grow slowly to the year 2000, then grow rapidly to 39 million by 2015—a 78 percent increase in less than three decades. The average income of households headed by "older" Americans is 10 percent higher than the national average. Households headed by "older" Americans spend 7 percent more than the average household.

> "They're a golden generation. They had the benefit of an extremely good economy, and that makes them unique," says Charles Longino, director of University of Miami's Center for Social Research on Aging.

> "Indeed, the generation of 'older' Americans now facing retirement is blessed because its careers prospered with the longest economic boom of the 20th century. Many of today's 50- to 64-year-olds reaped big economic benefits from the postwar boom. In the more difficult 1970s and 1980s, their homes, savings, and investments still appreciated handsomely. And they are the first generation to benefit from substan-

tial pension plans and generous hikes in federal benefits for the elderly. For these reasons they are retiring
early. The percentage of men aged 55 to 59 who are in
the labor force dropped from 89 percent in 1970 to 79
percent in 1986."

Their lifestyle focus—health, self-fulfillment, a broad
spectrum of social activities, comfort, and what to do with
their increasing spare time—has prompted some advertisers to
refer to the 50- to 64-year-olds as "suppies" (senior urban professionals) or "opals" (older people with active lifestyles). As
they grow a bit older, they become "rappies" (retired affluent
professionals).

Men and women in this age group are, in many ways, at
the high point in their adult lives. The children are grown, the
mortgage is paid, and they have the highest discretionary income of any age group. This particular cohort is better educated and more affluent than their parents were at the same
age.

"With fewer expenses, higher incomes and impending retirement, 55- to 64-year-olds will feather their nests. Leisure
activities and products such as golf clubs and vacation condominiums will grow in popularity as this age group grows in
size. The financial services industry will be in an especially
good position to cash in on the incomes of this age group.
Householders in their final decade of work are concerned
about postretirement income." So says Joe Schwartz, writing in
American Demographics.

■ **The "elderly" (age 65 to 74):** Are the second largest mature
segment, at 17 million. While this group will hardly increase
at all through 2000, it will grow rapidly after that, for a total
gain of 45 percent between 1987 and 2015. The average income
of elderly Americans is only two-thirds of the national average.
They spend only 72 percent of the average.

The major source of income for this group is Social Security and other retirement benefits. But the elderly receive 80
percent more income than the average from estates, trusts, divi-

dends, and rentals. The value of their assets is almost 21 percent greater than the average.

Dychtwald notes that because many in this group have been removed from the activities of the workplace for some time, they are very sensitive about being excluded from society. They most definitely do not want to be "put out to pasture" by the young. Many men and women in this age bracket (as in the "aged" grouping discussed below) have active social and friendship networks and often remain quite involved in the community. The death of close friends or loved ones, likely during this period, can be very unsettling. And at this stage of life, the number of female-headed households begins to climb.

■ **The "aged" (age 75 to 84):** Totaled nearly 10 million in 1987. This group is projected to grow quickly, reaching 12 million by 2000, then grow slowly, numbering only 12.5 million by 2025.

By the time they reach 80 + , two-thirds of the aged population is female. Although some 80 + men and women remain active in the community, and a few are still working, most have retreated to a more reserved life of daily self-care and contact with a small group of family and friends.

■ **The "very old" (age 85 and over):** Are the smallest but most rapidly growing segment of mature Americans. In 1987, there were 3 million. This group should grow to 5 million by 2000 and to 7 million by 2015.

Households headed by people age 75 and older receive only half of the average household's income. This group's income from estates, trusts, dividends, and rentals is more than twice the average. The aged and the very old have assets with a value 5 percent above the average.

The over-50 group is becoming the largest economic group in the United States. At 62 million nationally, they are almost as numerous as the baby boomers, who are placed at between 68 and 77 million, depending on who's counting who. The over-50 group controls 50 percent of the discretionary income in the United States and 77 percent of the financial assets.

How do you pinpoint the geographic clusterings of more affluent older Americans? Longino has researched two key questions: How many retired people are affluent and where do they
live?

He suggests that there are two key groups of relatively affluent retired Americans: the *comfortably retired* and the *pension elite*.

The **comfortably retired** live in households with incomes
more than twice the poverty level. This group includes most
older Americans who have discretionary income. The comfortably retired receive money from three sources: Social Security,
pensions, and assets.

Generally, the share of the retired who are "comfortable"
is greatest among those age 55 to 64 (59 percent), and drops in
the older age groups. Only 38 percent of people age 75 and
older are comfortably retired. Much of the worklife of those in
the oldest age group occurred before World War II, when the
workplace offered fewer and lower retirement benefits. Most
Americans now age 75 or older were retired by 1970.

The **pension elite** have a different age distribution. Few
persons under the age of 62 get Social Security checks, and
most people in the oldest group do not have income-
generating assets. The pension elite are clustered in the 65 to
74 age group, with 12 percent falling into this category. Nine
percent of those age 75 and older and only 5 percent of those
age 55 to 64 are members of the pension elite.

■ **Definite geographical clustering exists.** Nearly 15 million people are comfortably retired in the United States, and another 3
million are among the pension elite. California has over 1.6
million of the comfortably retired, followed by New York and
Florida, with more than 1 million each. The same three states
each have over 200,000 of the pension elite. Pennsylvania
ranks fourth in both categories.

Proportions tell another story. While only 59 percent of retirees age 55 to 64 fall into the comfortably retired category nationally, more than 66 percent live in Connecticut, Hawaii,

Maryland, Nevada, New Jersey, and Washington. Just over half (51 percent) of Americans age 65 to 74 are comfortably retired, but more than 60 percent fit this description in Connecticut, Florida, Hawaii, Nevada, and New Jersey. Only 38 percent of retirees age 75 and older are comfortably retired, yet at least half have achieved this level in Hawaii, Arizona, and the District of Columbia, with Florida and New Jersey not far behind.

What do these states have in common? Arizona, Florida, Nevada, and New Jersey are resort and retirement states. Connecticut is home to a large number of retired executives. Hawaii has a large Asian population, and older Asians are more likely to live with their extended families than other Americans. This gives them a big advantage in Longino's economic measure, which is based on total household income.

The states with the largest shares of retirees in the pension elite form a similar list. Connecticut, Pennsylvania, Michigan, Arizona, Oregon, and Washington have the highest proportion of retired in the pension elite in all three age groups. Fully 18 percent of 65- to 74-year-olds in Connecticut and Washington, for example, are in the pension elite. Florida, Maryland, New Jersey, and Wisconsin also have large shares of the pension elite in two out of three retired age groups.

As the baby boom ages, older Americans will be better educated and more affluent. They will have fewer relatives, two or more incomes, multiple pensions, better retirement plans, and better health. They will live longer, retire earlier, and be more concerned with the quality of life than are today's mature Americans.

MARKETING KEYS FOR REACHING OLDER AMERICANS

■ Work the Marketing Niches

Jeff Ostroff suggests that our aging population has seven promising "niches of need." These needs are 1) the home, 2) health care, 3) leisure time, 4) personal and business counseling, 5) educational services, 6) financial products and services, and 7) products that combat aging. Part 3 addresses demographically driven marketing strategies for these niches.

■ Avoid Negative Myths

The major problem in marketing to older Americans is that our culture is deeply gerontophobic. Dychtwald notes that "We have a fear of aging and a prejudice against the old that clouds all our perceptions about what it means to grow old in America."

Dychtwald lists six prevalent negative myths and stereotypes that blind us:

Myth 1: People over 65 are old.

Myth 2: Most older people are in poor health.

Myth 3: Older minds are not as bright as young minds.

Myth 4: Older people are unproductive.

Myth 5: Older people are unattractive and sexless.

Myth 6: All older people are pretty much the same.

■ Market Positively

Modern Maturity* has created a handbook, "How to Advertise to Maturity," to help marketers develop positive advertising communications to people age 50 and over. *Modern Maturity* notes that "there are no rules or absolutes, because mature America is a highly diverse population group with varying resources and a broad spectrum of interests. lifestyles and opportunities." However, the handbook does make six broad suggestions:

---

*The American Association for Retired Persons (AARP), the second largest membership group in the United States, publishes *Modern Maturity* magazine, with a circulation of over 17.4 million.

● **Don't make a long story short.** "Give them the ingredients. The warranties. The test results. Mature Americans are experienced shoppers who've learned from a lifetime of buying experiences. They've bought their share of 'lemons.' Now they take the time to analyze. Evaluate. They won't make a buying decision based on 15 television seconds. To get the full story, they'll hear you out, and read every word of copy that gives them the straight scoop. Don't sell them short. They are intensely interested in your new products, but before they buy, they need the compelling reasons why. The more you give, the better."

— *Translation: Are you communicating?* Use longer letters, case examples, and testimonials. Provide facts and figures along with a narrative. Consider following up with phone calls for higher-ticket items. Chapter 16 offers several specific suggestions.

Be sure to increase type size in your ads, brochures, and catalogs. After age 40 eyes can use some help.

Many older Americans welcome your mail. A wistful comment to the *New York Times* from an 80-year-old woman: "My personal correspondence has dwindled because many of my old correspondents are dead, and my children are busy with their own affairs. The solicitations fill the gap."

● **Take off 15 years. At least.** "They look and act many years younger than their mothers and fathers did at age fifty, sixty or seventy. Proper nutrition, a zest for fitness and a more active lifestyle have greatly extended the vital years. The lesson to marketers? Talk to a person, not a birth date. Enjoy their continued youth with them. How should you cast them in your advertising? Show them looking and behaving a good fifteen years younger than preceding generations did at the same age. See them as they are."

— *Translation: Are you using appropriate role models?* Mature Americans are attractive. Use photographs that emphasize vitality. Use situations that are active. Robert B. Maxwell, AARP vice president, notes that while the young are getting older, "the old are getting younger. The 70-year-old today is more like

Photograph courtesy of *Modern Maturity* magazine.

the person of 50 twenty years ago. We have not yet found the fountain of youth, but research has shown that healthy older people can enjoy most of their mental and physical abilities, and even improve on them."

Lear's, a glossy publication for "the woman who wasn't born yesterday," praises over-40 women as "today's sanest, most creative, interesting Americans" whose "lives are changing, almost certainly for the better. . . . We have nothing to lose but our follies and nothing to gain but our lives."

Gwyneth Gamble Booth, public TV news anchor in Portland, Oregon, said, "On my 50th birthday I felt wonderful. I don't have a hang-up with my age. I would like to think I can be alluring at 65 or 75."

And Gloria Steinem, on being asked how she felt on turning 50, said, "It feels a lot like what 40 used to feel like."

Use appeals which leave autonomy and independence intact. Use the term "older Americans," "mature Americans," or "aging," rather than "elderly" or "senior citizens." And say "50 years or over" rather than "or older."

● **Don't put them all on a diet.** "Mature America relishes food. They know how to cook and they do. A special pleasure is preparing meals to nurture family and friends. Most of them love company and give high priority to entertaining. Having family and friends over is a way of life."

— *Translation: Appeal to all the senses when marketing to older Americans.* Good companionship, leisure activities, and entertainment are important. Mature Americans are major purchasers of shoes for walking, running, tennis, and aerobics. They climb mountains and enjoy active travel.

Grand Circle Travel, a Boston tour company, targets people age 50 and over for "extended vacations" of up to 26 weeks. A majority of their customers are age 65 and over. More than half are college educated, and their annual incomes exceed $25,000. To attract potential clients, they offer—via direct response coupons—a free brochure, "Going Abroad: 101 tips for mature travelers."

Marketing to mature audiences requires respecting their preferences. For example, the Portland Home and Garden Show traditionally opened at 6 p.m. on a Thursday. In 1988, the opening hour was set at 11 a.m., and attendance went up 1,500 over the same Thursday the previous year. Older Americans made the difference.

Nostalgia isn't limited to boomers: Bring back the good times and great songs of the '40s and '50s. Use these themes in your advertising, your in-store displays, and for give-aways. Consider a popular older spokesperson to represent your business to the public.

● **Keep a sense of humor.** "The kids are through school. Often pressures have lessened. There's more time to laugh. Even at themselves. Life isn't all seriousness. Keep it on the light side. A smile is better than a frown. Show warmth and humanity. Picture them laughing with friends. They are often at their happiest experiencing the joy of children and the special joy of grandchildren. Weave your product into their lives, but remember; most of them are just like their own younger selves, but more relaxed now, with time to smile. Time to have a sense of humor."

— *Translation: Market positively!* If yours is a product or service aimed at youth, think multigenerationally. Grandchildren can be your consumers; grandparents the customers. Grandtravel, a Chevy Chase, Maryland, travel operator, specializes in trips for grandparents and grandchildren. Their Kenya safari includes an escort prepared with stories, games, and projects to keep kids entertained. It is not cheap: currently the 15-day vacation costs $4,255 for adults and $3,725 for children under 12. (Specific marketing suggestions for those in travel and leisure are given in Chapter 14.)

Often those involved with health-related or financial products and services invoke terms of "doom and gloom" in their marketing. Chapters 13 and 15 provide alternative marketing ideas.

● **Don't take the romance out of life.** "There's never been more time for romance. Weekends aren't always with the kids. Dinner together is no longer a sometimes thing. Many are getting to know each other all over again. You may visualize older age as drab when it's often candlelight."

— *Translation: Assume there is a partner.* Especially for large purchases, be careful to include "the significant other" in discussions and demonstrations. Even when older Americans are not married, many enjoy active relationships.

Romance at later ages also brings with it concerns for protecting assets. Sensitive financial planning advice may be welcomed by the entire family. Chapter 14 expands this idea.

● **Plan for their future.** "New seeds are planted. New ideas take root. At 50 and over, many of life's adventures are yet to be lived. Plans that had to be postponed can now be activated. Back to school? Hundreds of thousands of people 50 and over return to college every year. Show that they can, and are, continuing to build, learn and grow. Depict them expanding their horizons, learning new skills. For more and more Americans, 50 and over is the jumping-off place for a new lifetime."

— *Translation: Retirement does not mean vegetating.* Older Americans look forward to new opportunities to learn, work, and be of service. Are you ready for them? Chapter 12 explores how education is becoming a lifelong objective.

Eckerd College, a small liberal arts school in St. Petersburg, Florida, began the Academy of Senior Professionals in 1982 to expose students to the experience afforded by the older community. The academy has grown to nearly 200 members and associate members. The school benefits as much as the community; many of the participants in the Academy are professionals who have been high achievers and wish to continue being productive. They teach seminars, assist younger students, and form a strong relationship with their adopted college.

■ **Target differently to the "older," the "elderly," the "aged," and the "very old":** A caution must be expressed in reviewing *Modern Maturity*'s upbeat marketing commentary. While the "new" mature American—and the aging baby boomer—may continue the affluent lifestyles they enjoyed in earlier years, many of the "oldest" of Americans—a large proportion of those currently retired—are hard-pressed for cash.

"Not all retirees are as affluent as they may appear from the cars they drive or the homes they live in," warns Marshall Sewell, a retired fund raiser from New Jersey. "Some may have been forced into early retirement without the 'golden parachutes' their board chairmen enjoyed. Others may have had their finances depleted through family illnesses. Still others, members of the 'sandwich generation,' may be babysitting their grandchildren in the evening, then visiting an aged parent in the nursing home (and paying for the care) the next morning."

■ **Some older persons resent the positive picture of aging being painted.** A *Modern Maturity* reader writes:

> My siblings and I are tired of the bouncing, hyperactive "seniors" pictured in your pages. *Seniors*, my fat foot! Life is not all that blissful when you hit the mid-70s. Engines knock and wheels wobble. The M.D. prescribes a hearing aid; says your cataract can be removed "when ripe" but it may be a little late to do

something about your bunions; is jovial about your various operation scars; says you've recovered well from the Bell's palsy with just a slight facial distortion; your occasional dizziness and ocular migraine are nothing for you to worry about—you're tough, a survivor! Just like the golfers and mountain climbers in *Modern Maturity*! Me, I'd like some practical exchanges about ways of dealing with those wobbly wheels and knocking engines. "Golden years"? Phooey! Not inspiring—irritating! Give us a magazine about the realities of old age!

Remember: Each subgrouping within the older market differs both demographically and psychographically. Recognizing that the mature market is not monolithic can help you plan marketing strategies that appeal strongly to key older prospects. To successfully tap the rich potential of the mature market, today's marketers must look to both the present and the future.

In the future, the mature consumer will change. As the baby boom ages, older Americans will be better educated and more affluent. They will have fewer relatives, two or more incomes, multiple pensions, better retirement plans, and better health. They will live longer, retire earlier, and be more concerned with the quality of life than today's mature consumer.

In the decades ahead, older Americans will not remember the Great Depression. They may be more willing to enjoy the lifestyle that their assets—and not just their income—can support. . . . Age, not youth, is where the action will be for the foreseeable future.*

---

*William Lazer & Eric H. Shaw, writing in *American Demographics* on *"How Older Americans Spend Their Money."*

CHAPTER EIGHT

Targeting Working Women

UNDERSTANDING THE CHANGING ROLE OF WOMEN

THE INFLUX OF WOMEN INTO the work force has been called "the most significant societal change of the twentieth century." From statistically insignificant numbers, women in our work force have grown to 53 percent. Today, about 74 percent of men work. But 79 percent of women with no·children under eighteen work, as do 67 percent of women with children.

Women will account for about 63 percent of new entrants into the labor force between 1985 and the beginning of the new century. And while large numbers of women still labor in the "pink collar ghettos" with lower paying salaries, women are beginning to take their place in technology-intensive professions, and are moving up the management tiers.

MAJORITY MILESTONES FOR WOMEN

When more than half of any group does something, or has a particular characteristic, it's considered a milestone. From then on, in this case, we can say "most women work in the paid labor force" and "there are more female than male college students."

Here are milestones Peter Francese, publisher of American Demographics, has identified for women.

- Women became a majority of the total population in 1946.

- Women became the majority of U.S. college students in 1979.

- More than 50 percent of all women were in the paid labor force for the first time in 1979.

- More than 50 percent of married women were in the paid labor force for the first time in 1980.

- More than 50 percent of all married mothers with children under age 6 were in the paid labor force in 1984.

- Because women have been entering the labor force with such speed (they have accounted for more than half of all labor force growth since 1972), as of 1987, more than 50 percent of the entire U.S. population is now in the labor force.

In reality, these milestones may not fully reflect the scope of women in our workforce. Horst Stipp, Director of Social Research at NBC, has suggested that because women enter and exit the labor force frequently, standard statistics may understate women's work patterns dramatically. In fact, Stipp suggests that "among a target group dear to the hearts of marketers—women aged 18 to 49—about 90 percent can be considered part of the labor force. The 'typical housewife' has become rare indeed.

DRAMATIC DEMOGRAPHIC CHANGES

The combination of postponed or no marriage, increased education, and commitment to a "career" rather than "work," has enabled women to establish independence from their families. Women on their own will represent one in six households

> High-achieving women have made great commitments to advance their careers:
>
> - 28 percent of the MBAs awarded in 1982 were to women (up from 2 percent in 1962)
>
> - 60 percent of executive women have no children (compared to 3 percent of their male counterparts)
>
> - 4 out of 10 women don't marry at all (both from choice and lack of it)

through 2001. When the baby boomers start to retire in 2010, that proportion is likely to grow. Two-thirds of women living alone are age 55 or over, and a growing share of women are never-marrieds. As a result, the average woman has fewer children today than women had a generation ago.

By taking their labor out of the delivery room and into the marketplace, women have set in place a dramatic change in our society, the consequences of which will affect everyone.

CHANGING ATTITUDES

The demographic changes being accompanied by a resounding change in attitudes:

■ **While 94 percent of women continue to endorse marriage,*** they perceive it as a responsibility to be shared between both partners. Similar roles are the ideal, with husband and wife working to contribute earned income and sharing homemaking and child-rearing responsibilities. This has strong implications for those dealing in home-related products and services. See Chapter 11 for suggestions.

---

*A recent Virginia Slims poll

■ **Changing attitudes are also propelling women into the ranks of business owners, and top company leadership positions.** More women are prepared to run companies than ever before, since millions of them have progressed through the ranks in fields that were once male-dominated. To understand the implications for your organization, see Chapters 20 and 21.

WHY TARGET WOMEN?

There are four major reasons for your marketing efforts to seriously target women:

■ **Women have increasing economic power.** As a result of the growth of women-owned businesses, and the increase of executive and professional women in traditional organizations, women are accounting for a growing share of consumer spending. Since 1970, the median income of all American women age 15 and over (those who work and those who don't) has increased by 16 percent, after adjusting for inflation. By 1986, women's average hourly earnings were 68 percent of men's, up considerably since 1970.

■ **Women have greater potential for major purchases in their own right.** Increasing numbers of women are capable of making major purchases from income. While only 6 percent of those earning $50,000 or more in 1980 were women, by 1986 the numbers had doubled to 12 percent. Many of the women earning higher salaries are single, or married without children, and have higher disposable incomes.

(The higher a women's educational attainment, the fewer children she has had, or expects to have. It also is more likely that she plans to have no children. For example, some 20 percent of women with five or more years of college do not plan to have children, compared to only 7 percent of women who have not completed high school.)

■ **Women outlive men.** At age 65 to 69, there are 83 men for every 100 women. By age 70 to 74, there are 74 men for every 100 women. By age 75 to 79, the number of men per hundred women drops to 64. It drops again at age 80 to 84 to just 53. And at age 85 and over, there are just 40 men for every 100 women.

Women control the disposition of their own estates, and often that of the spouse as well. Obviously, this has significant marketing ramifications for financial planners. However, it would be short-sighted not to recognize that women's longer lifespans make them key consumers for those products aimed at older Americans. Healthcare, alternative living arrangements, personal shopping and errand services, meals for one, leisure activities such as cruises—businesses offering these services should target older women.

■ **Women have a new awareness of the power of the dollars they control.** Married women, as their roles have shifted from dependent homemakers to equal partners, or even to major providers of their family's incomes, are increasingly making the purchasing decisions for larger items, as well as the day-to-day items and services their households consume. And single women are no longer postponing purchasing decisions to a married future. They buy homes, cars, and other high-ticket items routinely. Women choose to buy from organizations that treat them with respect.

MARKETING KEYS FOR WORKING WOMEN

■ **Show women in your advertisements.** Have photographs of both women and men. Show some women without men. Show women in their late thirties and forties, as well as more mature examples. But don't be offensive. Appealing to women as women, just like targeting specific racial or ethnic groups, must have a logical context and sensitivity.

■ **Establish your credentials with working women.** Make your business inviting. Open early and close late. Put a "child proof" area aside for those who bring youngsters with them. Support local women's organizations and causes in your community. Being more "inner-directed" than males, women are likely to support businesses that support projects where the individual makes a difference. Humanities, health, social services, and the arts hold special appeal. Chapter 18 suggests public/private partnerships which work.

■ **Be sensitive to areas where women have been overlooked.** Make sure you include both the husband and wife in discussions and demonstrations, especially for major purchases.

■ **Be patient.** Recognize that many women are more concerned with their ability to replace assets than are men. Making a major purchase triggers anxieties. Be prepared to spend time with your customer.

■ **Recognize that working women are not a homogeneous group. Segment out groupings of particular interest to you.**

● **Use demographics of marital history, income, age, and lifestyle.**

Martha Taylor of the University of Wisconsin proposes the following "unscientific groupings" of women:

- Married/Widow—wealthy, older, 75 +

- Married/Widow—wealthy, younger, 45 +

- Married/Widow—well to do, never worked at a professional job

- Married/Widow—well to do, works/worked at a professional job

- Single—wealthy, older, 75 +

- Single—wealthy, younger, 45 +

- Single—well to do, never worked at a professional job

- Single—well to do, works/worked at a professional job

While Taylor's segmentation is demographically determined, it is logical to assume differing attitudes, values and lifestyles based on age and history of working/nonworking. This can be used by the marketer to create a "we" feeling.

● **Understand differences *between* working women.** The *Moving Target** provides a breakdown predicated on attitudes towards working. The woman who sees herself as in a career (22%), is very different from the woman who views work as "just a job" (37%); they are different from those who stay at home by choice (28%), versus those who plan to work (13%). Women who work for self-esteem, achievement, or identity needs are very different from those who work from economic necessity, or the difference a second paycheck makes. How you appeal to them must differ too.

Author Rena Bartos finds "a curious gap between the realities of social change and social trends reflected in most marketing plans, and in the advertising that expresses those plans." Outmoded assumptions about women lead to marketing underachievement.

She suggests that we must constantly reexamine the assumed target, noting that attitudes, values, and lifestyles are in flux for many women. The late 30s through mid-40s are a time of reevaluation, which can signal changes in priorities.

● **Access subgroups of women as prospects.** Bartos also urges a continuing reevaluation of the market potential of new target opportunity groups. Women, for example, are heavily represented in minority populations. The strong family and

---
*The first comprehensive marketing study on working women, authored by Rena Bartos, President of the Rena Bartos Company, New York.

community ties of Hispanic-Americans suggest that Hispanic women will pass their product/business loyalties to their children and grandchildren.

And minority women are gaining economically. From 1965 to 1985, the number of black women enrolled in college rose from 148,000 to 600,000, a 300 percent increase. (This gain is *not* paralleled for black men.) A corresponding occupational distribution—employed black women in service jobs dropping from 42 percent to 30 percent, and an increase of black women employed in technical, sales and administrative occupations (from 26 percent to 38 percent)—has occurred, with an accompanying increase in income. With female Hispanic-Americans increasingly attending college, similar gains for Hispanic women can be anticipated.

● **Older women prefer traditional approaches; younger women view themselves as more in control.** If you show women in your print advertisements, know whom you want to attract. The message "I belong" will only work when the role models parallel how a woman feels about herself, or wishes to perceive herself. If your audience is the mature widow who has inherited money, your photographs should show a background of home and family. Dress is more formal; makeup subdued. If your appeal is aimed at the career woman—self-made, probably younger and never-married—your photograph should use an active office background, or travel setting. Your model should wear either a business suit or leisure clothing. You may want to include a cordless phone, VCR, or computer: large numbers of younger, single women are Inner-Directed experientials known for their fascination with gadgets.

● **Younger, career-oriented women are likely to be offended by marketing approaches that suggest they need to be taken care of.** They want to see themselves as decision-makers, setting a course of action that secures their own future. Appeal to their need to control the future. Suggest several different options, but include female role model recommendations on each. Copy should be crisper, and graphics bolder.

Within every demographic segmentation—by age, sex, race or ethnic group; by income, education, or occupation; using household characteristics, residence or life cycle—women tend to be *the* target, either as direct consumers or as purchasers for others. Check your marketing plan for hidden biases, and audit your front line staff for unconscious patronization. No business—whether run by males or females—can afford sexism in the 1990s.

CHAPTER NINE

Introducing Baby Busters

CHERYL RUSSELL, EDITOR of *American Demographics*, sees trouble ahead for businesses. It's all because of the **baby bust**, the small group born between 1965 and 1976 who are now 14 to 25 years old.

Nestled between the baby boom and the baby boomlet, busters' demographics have resulted in fewer young adults to-

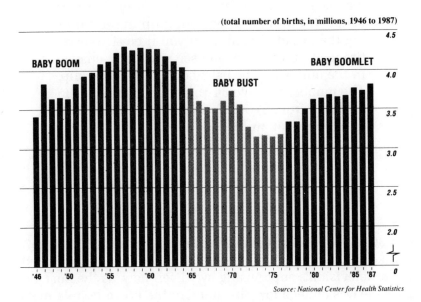

(total number of births, in millions, 1946 to 1987)

BABY BOOM

BABY BOOMLET

BABY BUST

Source: National Center for Health Statistics

day than at any time since 1973. Russell warns that during the 1990s, the ebb tide of the baby bust will drain the 25 to 34 age group. The oldest baby busters turn 25 this year, and 35 in 2000. Today there are 44 million people age 25 to 34. By 2000 there will be only 37 million, a 16 percent decline.

The drop in this age group could be even more dramatic for your business, depending on who and where your customers are. The number of whites age 25 to 34 will fall by 22 percent during the 1990s. The number of blacks, in contrast, will drop by just 8 percent. Eight states are projected to lose more than one-quarter of their 25- to 34-year-olds in the next ten years, according to the Census Bureau. Even California will see an 8 percent loss, while Florida will lose 7 percent. Alaska and Hawaii are the only states in which the number of 25- to 34-year-olds is projected to grow.

Few businesses will go unscathed. If your market is 25- to 34-year-olds, then business as usual will mean a 16 percent drop in sales during the decade ahead. And you'll be at your retirement party before you see much of a change in the numbers. The baby boomlet is just a blip. The number of 25- to 34-year-olds is projected to creep up from 37 million in 2000 to 38 million in 2010 and 39 million in 2020.

WHO ARE THE BABY BUSTERS?

Just 30 to 35 million people were born between 1965 and 1976. Unlike the boomers, the busters "grew up in relative obscurity under television's supervising eye. Even now, as the bust vanguard leaves college for jobs, none of the boom hoopla marks the milestone. They're the Lonely Crowd of the 1980s," according to Roper's *The Public Pulse.*

■ **They've been called the "Reagan Generation"**; compared to the older and larger baby boom generations, they are a very different type of American. They tend to be cautious, conformist, anti-intellectual and pessimistic: Many are fearful, frustrated, angry, and believe they will be exterminated in a nuclear war.

Research by the Roper Organization reveals busters to be more conservative than the previous generation. They appear to have little interest in championing causes, but the liberalizing events behind the Iron Curtain have caught their imagination. Sixty-two percent believe the government should make a major effort to combat racial discrimination, poverty, and ghetto problems, compared to 54 percent of Americans age 30 to 44.

■ **Busters are decidedly "pro-business,"** and more than three-quarters of them—compared to 69 percent of the baby boomers—have favorable opinions of large business corporations. This is even more impressive when you consider that 21 percent of young adults have a "highly favorable" opinion of large companies, compared to just 12 percent of the baby boomers now and the same number in 1978.

■ **They aspire to the traditional values of career, home, and family.** Many are the children of divorced or two working parents. While, on the one hand, they are even more accepting of dual-career marriages, they are also more inclined to plan for larger families than did the baby boom.

ECONOMICALLY BETTER OR WORSE?

Demographers are arguing over whether busters will have an easier time financially than did the baby boomers. There's less cohort competition for jobs, but the baby boom continues to compete for all but entry level positions. Many believe that "demographics are on their side"; the size of the labor pool will drop by an anticipated 23 percent by the turn of the century. Baby busters can afford to be picky with colleges and jobs.

Like boomers, busters are postponing marriage. They are staying in school longer and getting their careers underway. The number of young householders is shrinking by 8 percent—from 26 million in 1986 to 24 million in 2000. By the time the oldest baby buster turns 35 at the start of the new century, young householders should be fewer but more affluent than they are today.

Households Headed by Persons Under Age 35, By Income: 1986-2000

Income–1985 $ (for previous year)	Households (in thousands)			
	1986	**1990**	**1995**	**2000**
All households	25,913	26,786	25,380	23,853
Less than $10,000	4,734	4,574	3,985	3,446
$10,000-$19,999	6,574	6,308	5,441	4,652
$20,000-$29,999	5,904	5,909	5,338	4,738
$30,000-$39,999	4,103	4,423	4,278	4,001
$40,000-$49,999	2,237	2,575	2,747	2,836
$50,000-$59,999	1,137	1,323	1,467	1,590
$60,000-$69,999	736	948	1,116	1,266
$75,000 and over	488	724	1,008	1,324
Median Income	$22,790	$24,250	$26,120	$28,080

Source: *American Demographics*, October 1987.

Unfortunately, the bust has inherited the high cost of living—especially spiraling housing costs—fueled by boomer demands. For the first time in U.S. history, young Americans cannot necessarily expect more material achievement than their parents attained.

And there's a lot of resentment towards the baby boom. Busters think the boomers took the biggest pieces of the pie and left them with the crumbs. Notes Albert Stridsberg, a Poughkeepsie, New York, marketing analyst:

> Their older brothers and sisters, the boomers, kept telling them about the enormous amounts of money they were going to make.
>
> But as busters emerge from college they're finding that there are few or no jobs, that they don't have as

wide a choice, and that the glamour industries are jammed with 25- to 35-year old baby boomers. Busters, too, are equipped with MBAs, but they're expected to take the kind of money offered 10 to 15 years ago....They're hostile and suspicious, because they feel cheated.

REACHING THE BABY BUST MARKET

American youth and young adults control $200 billion, mostly in discretionary dollars. They are your consumers of the twenty-first century. Youth oriented businesses need to reach them now; *all* businesses need to cultivate them for the future. But how do you market to baby busters?

Unfortunately, there isn't very much usable information. A study done in the late 1980s, by the advertising agency Berenter, Greenhouse & Webster of New York City, suggests dividing the buster market into three groups, ages 14 to 17, 18 to 21, and 22 to 24.

■ **The 18- to 21-year-old group is the most critical to reach.** "This is the only group you need to address," says agency president Barrie Webster. "If you successfully reach this fulcrum group, you ignite the fuse that sets the entire span on fire."

Eighteen- to twenty-one-year-olds are admired by teenagers for their independence, says Webster, while young adults admire them for their freedom. Because of this, 18- to 21-year-olds influence lifestyles and product preferences for the whole group.

Webster suggests targeting this middle group on campus: 40 percent are in college. Growing in popularity are the campus sample box giveaways, which provide a unique opportunity for businesses to cultivate the educated buster.

Radio is the best vehicle for reaching the buster. But unlike boomers, who have rock and roll in common, they don't have a common taste. The buster "Top 40" embraces everything from rap to reggae to New Age.

It's difficult to reach the 18- to 21-year-old through most media. They do not read newspapers or magazines often, and they watch an average of only 1.25 hours of television per week.

■ **If you're targeting teen busters, the largest number of children age 12 to 17 are found in households headed by 35- to 44-year-olds.** A question for the future: Will busters leave the nest to establish their own residences, or follow the boomer trend of returning home (dubbed "baby boomeranging")?

Teen busters watch more TV than other age groups, but they are also more likely to tune out commercials, according to Teen Research Unlimited. Two-thirds change channels during breaks and 89 percent fast-forward through commercials when watching videotaped programs.

Which types of TV spots do teens prefer? Funny or clever ones, not commercials that rely on celebrities or music. The least-preferred are those with a home-movie style or straight product demonstrations.

"Teens, probably more than any other consumer group, desire immediate gratification," says Peter Zollo, president of Teen Research Unlimited. "They prefer promotions that reward them at the time of purchase."

At this time, not enough research has been done on the buster generation, but the need for more is clear.

PREDICTING A BUSTER FUTURE

The Public Pulse concludes its report on busters with a list of questions: Will there be widespread disillusionment? Will young people turn against big business as the cause of their economic woes—or will they adopt an even more conservative outlook? What will happen to ambitious child-rearing plans if they cannot be supported by personal finances? As consumers, will the baby bust turn to *affordable* material goods— VCRs, designer clothing—as substitutes for big ticket items they cannot afford, like homes and automobiles? Or might they be saved in the end by a real estate glut and plunging home prices?

The Roper Organization concludes—as must we—that "as provocative as these questions are, their answers remain uncertain—pending the maturation of the Reagan Generation."

PART III

PICKING THE BETTER BUSINESS NICHES
OF THE 1990s

As important as demographically driven marketing is, it makes an assumption that you are in the right business. No matter how good your product or service, it's not likely to succeed if your business is obsolete.

Chapter 10 recaps the overall demographic trends by age, race/ethnicity, household, and geography, then offers some business-oriented predictions based on anticipated results from the 1990 census and the work of respected forecasters.

Numerous publications address trends, forecasting, and predictions. There is strong concensus that five "most likely to succeed" business niches are: the home, education, health and fitness, leisure, and financial products and services. Chapters 11 through 15 explain why these areas should fare especially well in the 1990s, and how you can successfully position your product or service.

Predictions to Help You Pick Your Niche

*T*HE 1990 CENSUS WILL PROVIDE businesses with essential refined demographic information. But, cautions *American Demographics*, don't wait impatiently by your mailbox. The completed analysis of census data will most likely take the entire decade.

You can anticipate the 1990 census analysis. After all, the 1990 census can only count the 250 million bodies that already exist. There should be no surprises, only confirmation of what we've been tracking through the 1980s.

The basic demographic trends that emerged from the 1980s can be used to make some predictions for the 1990s.

AGE TRENDS

■ **Nationwide, youth is not dominating anymore.** Although traditionally a population has a lot of children and young adults, a middling number of middle-aged people, and fewer elderly, by the year 2000 we will have roughly the same number of people at all ages.

Each group will expect to have its needs met, a challenge and an opportunity for businesses. But whether you are a national chain, or a business with just one location, understanding the *geographical distribution* of age groups will be necessary to tailor your marketing appeals properly.

Population Distribution by Age

Age	1980 (%)	1990 (%)	2000 (%)
0-24	41.4	36.0	33.9
24-49	32.7	38.3	37.6
50 +	25.9	25.7	28.5

Source: 1980 U.S. Census

■ **Nationwide, the number of 25- to 34-year-olds is projected to drop 15 percent** by the turn of the century. Only Alaska and Hawaii will have more 25- to 34-year-olds in 2000 than in 1990. Generally, the Sunbelt states—California, Nevada, Arizona, New Mexico, Texas, Florida, and Georgia—will show the least shrinkage. The smaller "baby buster" cohort means increased competition for their services as workers. It also suggests a smaller market for products and services associated with young adults—household furnishings and children's products and services, for example. The number of low-income households among this age group will decline. The biggest change forecast for this age category is that more households will have incomes between $60,000 and $75,000.

Smaller family sizes suggest a market for upscale family furnishings, clothing, and activities. And the "boomlet" children are likely to be given increased dollars to spend as they enter their teens.

■ **As the huge baby boom generation moves into middle age** during the 1990s, the nation can look forward to a drop in the use of recreational drugs and an upsurge in demand for such things as second homes, diagnostic health care, and financial services.

Products and services that help baby boomers resist aging will be especially "hot," according to Jeff Ostroff. He pinpoints:

- A growth in the popularity of weekend vacations, along with the rise in interest in fitness activities, will create a huge market for **"wellness weekends."**

- The quest for social fulfillment in the later years, along with the fitness movement, will create a boom in 45 + sports leagues and **group activities** such as bowling, volleyball, golf, tennis for "doubles," bicycling, etc.

- The popularity of walking among 45 + ers in general, and older women in particular, will give **walking-oriented** products and services broad market appeal.

Ostroff also suggests that tomorrow's 45 + ers will line up for stylish-looking clothing which comfortably adorns their fuller figures.

■ **The population, as a whole, is aging.** The fastest growing age groups are the oldest ones. The 1990 census will show that 57,000 Americans have reached 100—a growth of 77 percent from the 1980 census. The oldest baby boomers turned 40 in 1986, ushering that massive generation into midlife. Youth age 10 to 24 fell because of the low birthrates of the 1960s and early 1970s; however, boomers are now having children and causing short-term growth in the number of children under age 10.

By 2000, the population will show a marked shift toward the elderly:

Total Population	1980 228 million	2000 268 million (projected)
Age 0–17	28.0%	24.5%
Age 18–24	13.3%	9.4%
Age 25–44	27.9%	30.2%
Age 45–64	19.5%	22.9%
Age 65 +	11.3%	13.0%

Source: U.S. Census Bureau, 1980

With older Americans living longer, a new wave of essential products and services are taking center stage. Horace B. Deets, executive director of AARP, suggests that products and services of the 1990s will focus on lifelong learning, medical marvels, changes in caregiving, and "smart" houses (dwellings that respond electronically to residents' needs).

Ostroff adds that travel and leisure activities (especially aimed at older, single adults), and financial services that help to "build and guard the nest" will also be growth opportunities.

MINORITY TRENDS

■ **Hispanics and Asians will far outpace the 10 percent population growth recorded since the 1980 census.** Notes *American Demographics:* "Adapting to cultural and language differences has been a major challenge in the 1980s, but it has also been profitable. Marketers have discovered that the demand for ethnic products and services, from guacamole to acupuncture, reaching far beyond narrow demographic niches."

■ **The proportion of whites is declining in every age group** while blacks, Hispanics, and Asians are increasing. Their different lifestyles, buying behaviors, and media preferences will have a profound affect on American business.

■ **The higher child-bearing rates for Hispanics and blacks mean youth will increasingly be minority.** Daycare, after-school care, camping, and weekend programs will be marketed in both Spanish and English to a less affluent audience. Packaging for children's toys, clothing, and furnishings will also reflect "minority" preferences.

■ **Women and minorities will be increasingly sought after as skilled workers.** Responsibilities, occupations, and opportunities will become more alike as our society accepts diversity as a positive force.

According to *The Numbers News*, the demographic trends shaping the 1990s point toward a more diversified consumer population. What's new is that formerly small groups are becoming large relative to what used to be the norm. Mass marketing will take on a different look as consumer marketers become more sensitive to:

- knowing who their customers are, what they are thinking, and what they want;

- caring for the consumer and about the consumer;

- breaking down stereotypes and taking advantage of diversity.

HOUSEHOLD TRENDS

The traditional family continues to decline: There are more single parent families, more people living together without marriage, more childless adults; the 1990 census will show that the range of household types continues to broaden.

■ **Women have become increasingly committed to the work force, and are less likely to marry and have children.** Although some marketers thought the women's labor force participation had peaked in the 1980s, *American Demographics* doubts the 1990 census will show a return to traditional family life.

Household Variety Is Increasing
(households distributed by composition)

	1990 (%)	2000 (%)
All households	100.0	100.0
Married couples		
w/o children	30.5	33.3
with children	25.5	20.1
Single parents	8.1	8.6
Living alone	24.7	26.3
Sharing w/others	11.2	11.7

Source: *American Demographics Household Projections, Number News,* January 1990.

■ **The family is back,** smaller and different than before. "Cocooning" before the entertainment center with gourmet snacks has led to a boom in catalog sales. And today's parents include children in more activities, making organized recreation like kiddie gyms and Club Med vacations a booming market.

■ **With both baby busters and baby boomers committed to two-career families,** time-poor families are ideal consumers for daycare (for both children and elderly parents), domestic help, personal shoppers, and organized leisure and health activities.

■ **Look for older moms.** People will continue to marry later and medicine will make it increasingly easier and safer for women to bear children in their 30s and 40s. Upscale maternity clothing, baby products, and nursery furniture will find a strong niche.

■ **Diversity is making the concept of a dominant spending group passe.** The middle-income household is vanishing. Household diversity will continue to polarize incomes. Trends in education will add to this polarization, as education determines economic opportunities. You'll need to market to specific subgroups.

GEOGRAPHICAL TRENDS

■ **Population and economic activity will continue to shift to-wards the south and west.** By 2000, the Northeast will have only 19 percent of the nation's population, barely half of the South's 36 percent, according to current Census Bureau projections. Employment firms, especially those specializing in retraining older workers, recruiting baby busters, and placing the handicapped and disabled will find their niche.

■ **More Americans will move than ever before.** Seventeen percent of us are living in a different home today than a year ago, according to the 1986 Current Population survey. Almost one in ten moves from one region to another, with the Northeast and Midwest continuing to lose migrants to the southern and eastern states. Young Americans move more often than older Americans. Do-it-yourself moving truck rentals, home furnishings, and portable storables should do well.

■ **The South and West continue to dominate population growth in the U.S.,** capturing nearly 90 percent of our nation's ten year population gain. The Northeast has become the least populous region of the country.

According to *The Statistical Abstract of the United States*, the Sunbelt will keep booming, while the Frostbelt will shrink. In the North, only New Hampshire will show growth.

■ **The Southwest is the place to locate your business,** according to the 1989 Arthur Andersen Enterprise Survey of emerging and owner-managed businesses. While the northeast, central and western states have seen a decline in the growth of sales, and the Southeast has held pat, sales in the Southwest have actually grown by 11 percent.

■ **Big cities began reversing the trend of population loss that prevailed in the 1960s through early-1980s.** Although twelve of the country's twenty-five largest cities continued to lose population, the gains of the other thirteen cancelled out the losses. New York, Philadelphia, and Boston grew along with Columbus, Indianapolis and Des Moines. Dallas, San Francisco, and Denver declined but Baltimore, Akron, Chicago, Milwaukee, the Twin Cities, and Kansas City held their own.

■ **Most cities will *add* people,** according to *The Kiplinger Washington Newsletter,* **over the next ten to fifteen years.** "Cities are shaping up; providing more jobs and easier commuting than suburbs."

OTHER FORECASTS TO CONSIDER

We've seen the trends predicted from the census data. Now, add the predictions of respected forecasters to this census-driven data. By adding lifestyle information to demographics, they try to anticipate the future. Often, naturally, they don't completely agree.

● **United Way's futurists** say these are the trends that will affect America's future:

- The childbearing of early baby boomers will end by 1991.

- White collar crime will increase.

- High-income households will grow faster than low-income households.

- The number of children in poverty will grow.

- A "conservative mood" will prevail, particularly among the traditional liberal 18 to 29 age group.

- There will be a revival of confidence in institutions and business.

- The above average growth of California and fifteen East Coast states will create a bicoastal economy.

- Corporations will continue to do cause-related marketing.

● **The Kiplinger Washington Letter**, in a special report on "Investments for Today and Tomorrow" suggests watching computers, office automation, robotics, consumer electronics, genetic engineering, telecommunications, and superconductivity. Home entertainment, travel and leisure industries, financial service companies, and home building/home remodelling industries also show promise.

● John Naisbitt and Patricia Aburdene, in **Megatrends 2000**, offer ten new directions for the 1990s:

- A Global Economic Boom

- Renaissance in the Arts

- The Emergence of Free-Market Socialism

- Global Lifestyles and Cultural Nationalism

- The Privatization of the Welfare State

- The Rise of the Pacific Rim

- The Decade of Women in Leadership

- The Age of Biology

- A Religious Revival of the Third Millennium

- The Triumph of the Individual

● **Thirty-one key trends** that will shape the future of American business were given in a special issue of Roper's *The Public Pulse*. "These trends cut across virtually every facet of American society and point to major changes in consumer lifestyles, working habits, public attitudes toward business, and political beliefs. These are the trends with true staying power—the harbingers of the emerging social and economic landscape in which American business will operate. These are not merely changes of degree but significant new departures in the way people look at their lives—and hence the products they buy, the services they use, the work that they do, and the major issues that concern them."

Here are all 31 trends, with explanations only when necessary:

- **Time Control**: Americans are increasingly placing a premium on time; seeking ways to segment their time, allocate it more efficiently, and stretch their leisure hours.

- **Component Lifestyles**: The trend is away from conformity and towards individualistic behavior. New and surprising combinations of consumer interests, spending patterns, and buying habits will be the rule rather than the exception.

- **Culture of Convenience**: All indicators point to growth of service businesses, and a spreading culture of convenience.

- **Home Shopping will Grow Dramatically**

- **Shopping Habits of the Sexes will Converge**

- **Home Entertainment will Escalate**

- **Market Segmentation in Physical Fitness Activities**: The "fitness market" is being divided into progressively smaller niches, as mass activities like jogging lose popular appeal and specialized fitness products and programs grow.

- **Dress for Success**: Small-scale clothing manufacturers with distinctive lines, boutique-type retail outlets, and large-scale manufacturers that can meet the demand for individuality and quality will flourish.

- **Spread of the Diversified Diet**: Consumers are not just eating better, they're eating differently.

- **Self-Imposed Prohibition of Alcohol**

- **The Lightest Drink of All**: Water

- **The Bifurcation of Product Markets**: High volume or high price. These strategies hold the best potential for future products.

- **Product and Service Quality**: Most important, if not everything.

- **Advertising and Marketing**: Heightened importance of visuals.

- **VCRs will Improve Image of TV**: Giving at least an illusion of control and selectivity.

- **Fragmentation of Media Markets**: More specialization of vehicles.

- **The Family is Back**: But in different forms.

- **New Employee Benefits for Two-Income Families**

- **Growing Appeal of Homework**

- **Older Americans**: The next entrepreneurs.

- **The Young American**: A new kind of conservative. Current Americans, between 18 and 29 years old, embody a unique blend of economic and political conservatism, while also being socially liberal.

- **Public Relations**: Tough times ahead for business. A deterioration of good will and increase of suspicion towards business will lead to massive swings in public sentiment on issues like regulation, taxation, and the environment.

- **The Personal Face of Business**: Business leaders with knowledge and charisma will be the strategy that counteracts lack of public support.

- **Improvements in Labor's Image?** Yes, but ultimately meaningless. Unless the labor movement responds aggressively to the changes in American society and its workforce, unions will risk becoming irrelevant.

- **Permanent Damage to Nuclear Energy Industry**: Growing environmental concerns in general, combined with recent disasters and an easing of concerns for energy independence and self-sufficiency, have retarded further developments in nuclear energy for the foreseeable future.

- **Government Regulation to Increase**: Business and government will be encouraged to become partners, not adversaries separated by regulatory barriers.

- **The Budget Deficit Won't Go Away**

- **Defense Spending More Vulnerable**

- **Reversal of Tax Cuts for Wealthy**

- **The Nation's Mood**: The new reality. Moving from the euphoria of the 1980s to relative austerity in the 1990s—a sobering up period. For marketers, this new mood possibility will restrain the level of consumer confidence and the willingness to incur debts for major expenditures.

All this information points to five specific business areas: the home, education, health and fitness, leisure time, and financial products and services. These should fare especially well in the 1990s.

CHAPTER ELEVEN

Home Sweet Home

*T*HE AMERICAN HOME AND the American dream are closely intertwined. The plaintive lament, "How can you be an adult when you don't own a house?" fairly sums up how most Americans feel.

Baby boomers fueled the soaring price of home ownership in the 1970s and 1980s. Over the decade that began in 1975, median prices for a first home rose 125 percent—from $27,100 to $61,000 in 1985.

Most real estate experts believe the heady appreciation of single-family housing associated with the 1970s and 1980s has ceased. The smaller baby buster market and the settling in of the aging boomers suggests there will be less need for homes in the 1990s—an average of 1.4 million starts versus the 1980's 1.6 million, according to Coldwell Banker's Robert Scanlan. A recent study* forecasts that home prices will decline 47 percent in real terms by the year 2007, as the wave of baby boom home buyers recedes.

But plenty of opportunity remains. If you are already involved with home building and home selling—or considering it for your business niche—strong potential exists for organizations and individuals who target home buyers using pinpoint refinement by area of the country, exact age, household type, income level, education, and ethnic characteristics.

*By Harvard researchers N. Gregory Mankiw and David N. Weil.

OPPORTUNITIES AND MARKETING KEYS FOR HOME BUILDERS/SELLERS

Over the next decade, the retirement housing market, now worth $3 billion per year, is expected to soar to $35 billion per year. As people live longer, the demand for real estate will reflect the buying power of an aging population.

■ **Age-segregated retirement communities and villages will continue to grow.** Before World War II, communities built around recreational facilities didn't exist. By 1984, some 2,300 had been built mostly in California, Arizona, and Florida. Today, more than a million people live in such complexes. Retirement communities offer residents a safe, controlled environment, plenty of friends and activities to share, and a supportive atmosphere.

Only 14 percent of older Americans plan to move following retirement. But that minority is more affluent and more active than the ones who don't plan to move. And, if mobility continues to rise with income and education, then retirement communities should boom in the coming decade.

The main thing that distinguishes movers from nonmovers is their attitude. They are dreamers. According to Dick Page,* Northerners who want to buy land in Florida are likely to be "pie-in-the-sky" people who hope for wealth."

In *American Demographics*, Page indicated that to reach this group, he

> buys lists of subscribers to magazines about gambling or sweepstake contests, and he gets lists of buyers or mail-order offers for "start your own business" plans or books like *The Lazy Man's Guide to Riches.* "You don't sell the land," he says. "You sell the dream."

> The best way to segment potential retirement migrants is by income. "If their annual income is between $25,000 and $50,000, you stress that

---

*President of Page & Associates, an advertising and direct marketing agency in Sarasota, Florida.

Floridians spend less on taxes, clothes, fuel, and recreation.'' At higher incomes, lifestyle is the key. And
as the prospect's income climbs, developers must target their pitch to specific interests. One of his clients
sent subscribers to *Golf* magazine a brochure that features a championship golf course. Another used a
list of northern boat owners for a brochure about wa-
terfront living. A third targeted pilots for a mailing
that mentions a nearby airstrip.

■ **Congregate care (in which residents have separate quarters
but share dining facilities and other amenities) and assisted
elderly housing will be very strong.** Especially among the
most elderly segment of our population, the aged cohort, lifecare and assisted residential care situations will grow.

Retirement Living Plus 24-Hour Care equals Lifecare. Developers such as the Marriott Corporation and the Forum Development Group have joined churches and universities to
meet a growing demand for housing combining an array of features. Individual homes and apartments, group dining, and a
broad spectrum of recreational activities, as well as fully
staffed medical and long-term care facilities, are all at one location.

So far, lifecare developments attract a population that is
more educated than average, somewhat better off financially,
less connected to family and children, somewhat older, and
more concerned about serious illness than are the more typical
retirement-community residents. Most of the growth will come
from developments aimed at the middle class, according to Jim
Sherman, a partner in Laventhol and Horwath, an accounting
and consulting firm that specializes in the lifecare industry.

Both retirement and lifecare communities should consider marketing to the baby boomer who often influences (or
makes) the decisions for her/his parent(s).

■ **Existing homes and new home designs will be adapted to an
aging population.**

*Remodelling businesses will expand as many older Amer-
icans opt to continue living independently.* Kitchens and
baths, especially, will be redesigned to help an aging popula-

tion continue to live safely and comfortably. In the kitchen, innovations will include lower counters with an open area underneath for wheelchairs, or a seated work space; lower pullout mixing centers with recessed bowl holders; large touch pads for telephones and microwave ovens for the visually impaired; and safety front controls on the cook top.

A market will exist for ECHO Housing (Elder Cottage Housing Opportunity), which solves the need for housing elderly parents near the adult child. Called "Granny flats" in Australia, where the idea originated, and "elder cottages" in the U.S., the prefabricated unit can, within hours, be placed in a backyard—complete with bedroom, living room, bathroom, utility nook, and kitchen. "Your significant elder has privacy and can come and go as he or she pleases, but is only steps away if the kids want to drop by and visit, if there's any problem, or if he or she wants to join you for dinner," says Ken Dychtwald in *Age Wave*.

ECHO cottages are catching on, notes Dychtwald. Currently, 13 percent of all prefabricated "manufactured" houses are located not in mobile home parks, but on the property of family and friends.

■ **Mature buyers will drive the affluent, upscale housing market.** People over fifty usually have completed the most financially demanding time of their lives, and often are ready to purchase higher priced real estate. Many are looking for down-sized housing, with more luxurious amenities and reduced upkeep and maintenance. Condominiums, cluster homes, and residential communities marketed to the mature buyer will grow in the years ahead.

■ **Mobil towns are merging retirement housing with travel.** According to a recent census, some 800,000 older households are set up in mobile homes. In 1984, 45 percent of all manufactured homes were owned by people over 50, up 4 percent from 1982.

Dychtwald describes "towns" formed in locations where large numbers of mobile seniors congregate for the winter. Entrepreneurs have taken the opportunities offered by this "snowbird invasion" to build golf courses and RV parks, and to provide needed services. These moveable towns are found in California, Arizona, and Colorado.

■ **There will be a smaller market of first-time buyers,** driven largely by the moving-on of the baby boomers and the smaller cohort of baby busters.

● **Prefabricated housing** will find its niche, especially among first time buyers and older buyers. Increased quality, variety of floor plans, and affordability of price suggest that many buyers who would not previously have considered a manufactured home are now fueling sales, especially in the Northwest and South.

● **The larger numbers of one-person, unmarried households** suggest a market for smaller, upscale condos and homes, as well as rental units. Amenities and security will be of special interest to these buyers, many of whom will be working women.

■ **As baby boomers move through their forties and into their fifties, they will look for housing that fits a changing lifestyle.**

● **Builders will cater to the move-up buyer.** Homes will be larger and fancier, with added space going to larger rooms, rather than more of them, says Salomon Brothers housing analyst Stephen Dobi. Middle-class homes will begin to resemble today's upscale houses: Lavish bedrooms with separate dressing areas; bathrooms that can accommodate Jacuzzis. Instead of a separate living room and family room, an open, high-ceilinged "great room" at the front of the house will become the gathering place for family and guests alike. At the same time, yards will shrink as land prices rise.

● **A second-home sales explosion** will translate to a *doubling* of sales. Increased leisure time is refueling interest in vacation homes. Those located within easy commuting range of the homeowners' primary residence and work location will be most appealing.

● **Buyers will choose to remodel,** rather than build. More than 70 percent of kitchen and bath construction is for remodelling, rather than new housing units.

Kitchen & Bath Business magazine expects a 13 percent increase in bathroom remodelling/replacing in 1990, a potential market of about 8 percent of U.S. households, spending an estimated $8.9 billion. The average age of someone redoing the bath is 41, with households headed by 30- to 39-year-olds making up a plurality (29 percent) of the market. The 40 to 49 age bracket accounts for 22 percent of the jobs, and the 50 to 64 age bracket is close behind at 20 percent. Almost 11 percent of the remodelling is done by households headed by someone 65 or older, while the under-30-year-olds make up 19 percent of the market.

While the kitchen is not as hot a candidate for remodelling as the bathroom, its potential is higher. As much as $19 billion annually is spent. The average kitchen remodeler is 42 years old. Almost 23 percent of kitchens will be redone by 50- to 64-year-olds, and 12 percent will be remodelled by households headed by someone 65 or older. The 40- to 49-year-old age group will account for 20 percent of the kitchen remodelling market; the 30- to 39-year-old bracket will make up 27 percent of the market. Almost 16 percent of the remodelling will be done by one-person households.

Empty nesters, parents with children who have moved away from home, often plan to improve the quality and usefulness of their current living quarters. Information gathered by the Spiegel Home Fashion Monitor noted that 45 percent of empty nesters constructed a guest room, 11 percent more garage space, 7 percent a new bedroom, 5 percent a sewing room, and 2 percent a viewing room.

■ **Working couples will want homes that help them manage their lives.** Imagine, says *U.S. News & World Report,* doors with locks designed for working parents. When a latchkey child comes home and unlocks the door, the key, encoded with the child's identity, triggers a phone call to Mom or Dad's office and a recorded message heralds the child's arrival. Such locks are on the drawing board.

The dramatic numbers of working women/mothers will create a market for secure housing in an environment where 70 percent of U.S. households have no one at home during the day. Many buyers will look for convenience: Stores on or near the premises, staff that will run errands, pick up drycleaning, let in a repairman.

Consider using psychographics to reach home buyers within demographic groupings. The VALS Typology (see Chapter 3) has been used successfully by a builder of single-family homes to market the same product—a 3 bedroom house with fireplace —to psychographically different audiences:

> **Commercial 1** shows an attractive couple, in their late thirties or early forties, sitting before a fireplace drinking Perrier. He's toasting her, she's toasting him. They congratulate each other on doing well and their choice of an "ABC" house. They reminisce about their experiences in the '60s when he wore a Nehru jacket, she had flowers in her hair, and they participated in peach marches and rallies. He notes, wryly, that now they "march with their checkbook." They agree that back in the early '70s—when jobs weren't easy to find—they always hoped that they would be able to have a quality ABC house. Who are they? A Societally Conscious couple: Affluent people who interpret their role in making the world a better place very personally, and who value quality in their possessions.

> **Commercial 2** features a young couple in their mid-twenties. He's fastening pearls around her neck as the doorbell rings. Their features and coloring suggest they might be Hispanic-Americans. She turns to him, eyes glistening, and whispers "They're here." In walk his mom and dad. Dad is paunchy with a sizeable beer belly. He wears a blue, short-sleeved shirt without a tie. Mom is formally dressed

with white gloves and a hat, carrying a black patent leather pocketbook. The young couple proudly show them through the house. Dad takes the young man aside and says, "Son, you know we would have helped if we could have." His son answers, "No problem, Dad. This is an ABC house; we were able to do it ourselves." Who are these people? Belongers: an Outer-Directed couple who bought into the American Dream and are working their way up.

Commercial 3 introduces an attractive mid-thirties woman wearing upscale leisure clothing and running shoes. Pulling up to the front of a house on a high-tech bicycle, she deactivates the alarm before entering. The house is filled with moving boxes. She picks up a cordless phone and calls her boyfriend. Inviting him to join her for dinner—marshmallows roasted in her new fireplace and microwaved main course—she admits she hasn't unpacked anything yet, but "loves her new ABC house." This ad is targeting Experientials, often single women, with its appeal to new technologies and recreation.

OPPORTUNITIES AND MARKETING KEYS TO CONSIDER WITHIN THE HOME

Masco, a respected manufacturer of furniture, accessories, appliances, and hardware, notes in its 1989 Annual Report that

> Population trends strongly enhance Masco's prospects for continued growth. The domestic baby boomers—some 77 million strong—represent a major segment of today's consumer and lifestyle demographics.

> By the turn of the century, the 35 to 54 age group will have expanded by more than 40 percent, and their discretionary income will have increased by an estimated 70 percent. In our judgment, demand for Masco products will be enhanced by this largest growth in households representing consumers who are better-educated, and at the peak of their earning capacity and inclination to spend.

■ **The baby boomers have become domesticated.** In many cases, having postponed marriage and family until they reached their thirties, boomers are now fuelling a "baby boomlet" of increased births. Mail order sales of birth gifts, apparel, mother's helper products, educational items, and toys reached $360 million in 1988, and launched a proliferation of children's catalogs—*Hanna Anderson, Childcraft, Disney, Talbots Kids,* and *Right Start.* Once relegated to the back of the department store, children's furniture, linens and room decorations are showing up at boutiques with upscale prices.

■ **Cocooning,** creating more "quality time" by retreating to and investing in one's home, is also boomer driven, but extends to all age categories. As a result, recreational and entertaining activities within the home are gaining more important roles in people's daily lives. Consequently, notes Masco, the home increasingly is becoming an even more important means of self-expression. Home furnishing products—furniture, wall and floor decorations, accessories, linens and beddings—all should do well in the 1990s.

The cocooning phenomenon suggests that many of the trends we will describe in the next chapters will find their resting place in the house of the 1990s. The trend towards eating in (for boomers) and/or multiple meal preparation suggests a change in how kitchens might be equipped; the interest in combating aging suggests increased interest in home gyms, exercising equipment and home saunas and whirlpools.

■ **The home office will grow in appeal.** A full 26 percent, or 25 million Americans, work at home full-time, and an additional 19 million work at home part-time.* This new way of work has been aided by affordable technology and a boom in information-based businesses. College-educated baby boomers are key to the trend which is fueling sales for overnight-mail services. The home market for personal computers, printers, modems, typewriters, FAX machines, telephones, and other home office supplies was an $8 billion business in 1988, and will double to $16 billion by 1993.

---

*According to the 1988 National Work-At-Home Survey by LINK Resources Corporation.

■ **The empty nest syndrome** often signals a remodelling splurge. The Siegel study determined that when children move out, parents spend an average of $719 redecorating a room. This is an important trend for the 1990s, as many older boomers will be moving into this lifestyle.

In concluding this chapter, we need to return to the opening caution: the mass market for housing is going, if not gone.

You'll need to pick up your niche and market specifically to the best prospects for it. Homebuilding, home remodelling, and home furnishing all will do well in the years ahead, as long as these businesses do their research. Whether your best customer is a boomer, a buster, or an older American, they'll be eager to make their residence a "Home Sweet Home."

CHAPTER TWELVE

The Business of Education

*I*NCREASINGLY, EDUCATION IS a
business. And, in the 1990s, it is big business. These trends are
responsible for making education a lucrative market:

- **Education is becoming a lifelong objective.**

- **Training and retraining will become increasingly important.**

  There will be a restructuring of the skills required in the workplace.

  AND

  The increasing demand for college-educated workers is outstripping the supply.

WHY IS EDUCATION BECOMING A LIFELONG OBJECTIVE?

■ **Learning is no longer exclusively the province of the young.**
In *Age Wave*, Ken Dychtwald notes that it has become increasingly common for middle-aged and older people to go back to
school. "Whereas education has been primarily geared to preparing the young for their lifetime careers, we are now coming
to think of learning as an ongoing, lifelong process. As the

pace of discovery quickens and our appetite for learning increases, we will find ourselves being retrained and retooled many times throughout our lives. In addition, as our commitment and need for learning expands, our interest in non-vocation-oriented education will increase as well."

Modern Maturity agrees. "The desire to learn is a joy that can continue through every age and stage of life. When you depict mature Americans, show them open-minded, and eager for new information. Mature America wants to be recognized as part of the world, not bypassed by it. Many enjoy the challenge of computers, mind-opening books, mind-boggling ideas, the newest in everything from nutrition to business management. Learning at 61 can be as exciting as it was at 16."

■ **Longer life will eliminate the rigid correlations between age and the various activities and challenges of adult life.** Fred Best, Ph.D., sociologist and futurist, believes we are moving away from a "linear" life plan, in which we obtain all of our schooling in youth, to a "cyclic" life plan, in which the idea of recurrent education throughout a longer and more healthy life is both reasonable and increasingly common.

■ **Continuing education helps those competing for professional recognition and economic rewards.** More than 23 million people spent $3 billion participating in more than 40 million adult education courses during the year ending May 1984, reports the U.S. Education Department's Center for Statistics. Almost two-thirds of the adult education courses were taken for job-related reasons. Half of the 40 million adult education courses were taken by students who wanted to advance in their current jobs, and 12 percent by those who wanted to get a new job.

Who are these students? 70 percent are aged 25 to 54. These are the career-building years when people are striving to get ahead. Sixty percent of the market are baby boomers. More than 55 percent were women. Another large grouping is younger baby boomers. Fully 31 percent of those who take part in adult education are professional or technical workers—more than double the share of these workers in the population as a whole.

WHY ARE TRAINING AND RETRAINING BECOMING INCREASINGLY IMPORTANT?

■ **The restructuring of skills required in the workplace as the jobs themselves are becoming more demanding and more complex is fueling a demand for retraining workers.** Rapid changes in the workplace have "upskilled" most job categories, according to a *Wall Street Journal* report, resulting in the nation's corporations spending some $30 billion a year on formal training to bring employees up to speed. By 2000, about 75 percent of workers currently employed will need retraining, according to the American Society for Training and Development.

Because of the incredible pace of technological and cultural change, the Rand Corporation, a futures-oriented think tank in Santa Monica, California, predicts that by the year 2020 the average worker will need to be retrained up to 13 times in his or her lifetime!

A growing concern is the increasing number of Americans unable to meet the minimum demands of their jobs, reports the *Wall Street Journal*. An estimated 23 million Americans are functionally illiterate, meaning that their reading and computational skills are very low. Some experts estimate that up to 65 percent of the work force is "intermediately" literate, meaning that this group can read at between fifth-grade and ninth-grade levels. That just isn't going to cut it when most workplace materials are written on the 12th-grade level.

■ **The demand for college-educated workers may outstrip the supply in the 1990s.** More and more corporations are seeking programs to allow their supervisory, middle, and top management personnel to improve and continue their education without sacrificing the productivity of the employee. Increasingly, employers are agreeing to reimburse or fund undergraduate and graduate degrees.

California Coast University, for example, markets its off-campus, accelerated degree programs to mid-career adults, noting in its catalog that "the true recognition of any degree comes from its voluntary acceptance by the business, professional and academic community. The University has on file many substantial, affirmative testimonials from graduates and leaders in business, industry, and in the professions. Many of these attest to promotions, new positions, and salary increases directly related to completion of a course of study and receipt of a Degree from the University.''

CHOOSING BUSINESS OPPORTUNITIES INVOLVING EDUCATION

■ **Package continuing and professional education programs.** The number of courses offered by businesses has increased faster than the number offered by any other provider—up 117 percent just since 1978. An incentive: among the *courses provided by businesses*, employers paid for 79 percent of those taken by men and 70 percent of those taken by women, compared to paying for 44 percent of the *adult education courses* taken by men and just 30 percent of the courses taken by women.

Or, aim at the mandatory continuing education (CE) market. Increasing numbers of states are requiring CE programs. Louis Phillips and Associates, continuing education and training consultants, notes that one-third or more professionals feel programs are "too basic" and "not relevant" to their needs and concerns. Program discontent seems highest in professions which operate continuing education much the same as ten to twenty years ago.

■ **Work with presentors to teach effective teaching practices.** Louis Phillips notes that few speakers know how to organize their presentations to involve their audiences. Too often, he suggests, program committees and decision-makers place too much emphasis on a speaker's credentials rather than delivery skills.

■ **Market lunchtime and "brown bag" lectures** to employers for increased productivity and goodwill. Such learning opportunities will be enthusiastically received by busy employees. At Tassani Communications Inc., a $25 million Chicago advertising agency, employees can attend "Food for Thought" brown-bag lunches and listen to lectures on stress management, crime prevention, and time management. Says CEO Sally Tassani, "People enjoy topics that help them in their everyday life —things we tend to neglect when working long hours. For a couple hundred dollars per speaker, it's an inexpensive way to make this a fun place to work and learn."

■ **Offer educational counselling services to adults looking to return to school.** The college counselling market for traditional 18- to 24-year-olds may be oversaturated, but many adults would welcome a service that provided information on nontraditional degree programs. With the increasing numbers of such programs available, employees—and employers—need a "one-stop" researching methodology.

■ **Offer remedial training programs in basic skills to businesses.** American industry has been slow to address this subsegment of the training market. The changing demographics of entry workers—a smaller pool, more heavily minority— suggest it will be a crucial area in the 1990s and into the next century.

■ **Target personal computer sales to older Americans.** While more than 20 percent of all U.S. households have home computers, only 9 percent of adults age 60 to 69 own them—a figure that drops to 3 percent for those 70 and older.

New computer-literacy programs designed with older persons in mind may soon change this. SeniorNET, the first national organization dedicated to bringing mature people into the information age, has trained thousands of older Americans to use computers. Once introduced to the power of the computer for networking and communication, older Americans enthusiastically use their machines for everything from educational forums to correspondence courses to researching hobbies.

■ **Target the baby boomlets' parents for youth educational sales.** Whether it's early reading clubs, language programs targeted

Now Available In Four Languages!

The BBC Language Course for Children
Only Seven Years Old*...
and She's Already Speaking French!

Give <u>Your</u> Child That Critical Early Advantage!

Now Available In French, Spanish, Italian or German!

Now Available for the First Time in the U.S.A.!

It's a scientific fact...and one of Nature's marvels. During the early years of childhood, the human mind is best pro-grammed for learning a language — any language.

That's why children learn so much more easily than adults, even *before* being able to read. They learn the same way they learned English — naturally — by listening, seeing, and imi-tating. In the international world our children will compete in — where so many Europeans and Asians start a foreign language early — a second language will be essential. Vital for competing with polished and accomplished peers.

Sample ages for beginning a second language**			
Japan	Age 8	France	Pre-School
Sweden	Age 7	Spain	Pre-School
Austria	Age 8	Canada	Pre-School

** Ages represent top schools and programs, compulsory language education usually begins several years later

From the BBC, World Leaders in Language Education
For the first time ever in the U.S.A., your child can learn French, Spanish, Italian or German using the most successful Language Course for Children ever created!

Muzzy, a unique video learning program, is produced by the BBC — the world's foremost teachers of language. Spe-cifically designed for children (pre-school through age 12), *Muzzy* uses color animation, enchanting songs, and charm-ing, involving characters (including *Muzzy* himself), and teaches children to absorb a new language the same way they learned English.

It's so easy and so much fun. In fact, most kids love to watch or listen over and over again, just like their favorite TV shows!

Complete Language Learning Course!
Everything needed for a child to master beginning French, Spanish, Italian or German is included. Four video cassettes. Two audio cassettes. An activity book and an excellent parent's instruction guide plus answer book. All in attractive, durable storage cases.

Through *listen-and-learn* and *see-and-learn*, your child will begin speaking a foreign language from the very first day! He or she can learn alone, or you can help and learn the language, too!

No Risk Guarantee!
Here is perhaps the greatest gift you will ever give your child...a second language. And at an astonishingly affordable price of just $145†, payable in four credit card installments. And there's no risk! If you and your child are not absolutely delighted, you may return the course within 30 days for a full refund. Order today from Early Advantage, 47 Richards Avenue, Norwalk, Conn. 06857.   †Plus $4.75 shipping/handling per course.

By exclusive arrangement with the British Broadcasting Co. A program proven with thousands of European youngsters. And the whole family can learn the language, too!

* Proven results for pre-school through age 12.   © 1989 MBI

The BBC Language Course for Children

Early Advantage   Satisfaction
47 Richards Avenue   Guaranteed
Norwalk, Conn 06857

For Fastest Service — Call Toll-Free: 1-800-367-4534

Yes! Please send me *The BBC Language Course(s) for Children* I have indicated. I understand only VHS format is available.

(Please check appropriate items.)
Language: ☐ FRENCH   ☐ SPANISH   ☐ ITALIAN   ☐ GERMAN

Name _____
              PLEASE PRINT CLEARLY
Address _____
City/State/Zip _____
Signature _____
              (All orders subject to acceptance.)

Charge each of four monthly $37.44* installments to my credit card:
   ☐ VISA   ☐ MasterCard   ☐ Diners Club   ☐ American Express

                                              Exp.
Credit Card No. _____ Date _____

☐ I prefer not to use my credit card and will pay by check. Enclosed is my deposit of $50* for each course. I will pay the balance of $99.75* as billed in three monthly installments.

*Includes one-time shipping/handling charge of $4.75. CT residents add 8%; TN residents add 7-¾% sales tax. Allow 2 to 4 weeks for shipment (4 to 6 weeks for German).

Reprinted with permission of Early Advantage (MBI, Inc.) ©1989.

at pre-schoolers, or home encyclopedias, competitive educated baby boomers will fuel sales to make sure their little ones follow in their tracks. In 1988, Americans spent over $500 million on encyclopedias.

And don't forget private education. There's been an upsurge in applications to private pre-school through high school institutions. Many boomers are reacting to their own overcrowded school day experiences, and searching for alternatives for their youngsters. Many private schools begin with modest start-up costs.

■ **Offer products and services that help people get in touch with their feelings.** The human growth movement may be fueled by boomers' reaction to technological intrusion. John Naisbitt suggests that baby boomers, especially, are receptive to products and services that counterbalance increasing technology. Courses and products that help them get in touch with their feelings and counselling services—both one-on-one and in group settings—will do well in the 1990s.

Can your business target the expanding field of education? If the examples given in this chapter suggest the answer is "yes," you've got an exciting future ahead.

CHAPTER THIRTEEN

Making Health a "Healthy and Wealthy" Business

Given only one choice, what is the most important thing in life: to be creative, famous, powerful, wealthy, or healthy? According to a recent poll conducted for the *Los Angeles Times*, Americans overwhelmingly chose good health. Fifty percent of all adults—43 percent of men and 55 percent of women—chose health and a long life, compared to 1 percent wanting power, 5 percent wealth, 6 percent creativity, 8 percent success, 10 percent a happy marriage and 16 percent to help others.

Today, health care accounts for about 12 percent of the gross national product, about double what it was in 1965, when Medicare was enacted. Between 1987 and the year 2000, national health expenditures should *triple*, to more than $1.5 trillion. That's the prediction of the U.S. government's Health Care Financing Administration.

■ **Not surprisingly, the health care market is booming.** The once-homogenous market for health services is fragmenting, as many services are developing along demographic lines of age, sex, lifestyle, and ability to pay. Women's care, family care, and geriatric care are but a few of the specializations now available.

While age has always been a determining factor in health care use, Richard K. Thomas and William F. Sehnert, writing in *American Demographics*, caution that "the differences in the lifestyle, socioeconomic status, and health care delivery preferences between the pre- and post-World War II groups are unique.''

> A key decision for entrepreneurs considering entering the health care market, and for providers already in the field, is whether to position their services to appeal to the more traditional health care market—roughly, those born before World War II or aged 45 and over— or to target the emerging modern market, primarily boomers and younger consumers under the age of 45.

THE EMERGENCE OF A DUAL HEALTH CARE MARKET

■ **Traditional health care consumers** are characterized by attitudes and values formed during the Depression and World War II: security, conformity, and authority. They favor the traditional approach to health problems, with its emphasis on pathology, technology, treatment and cure. "Good patients": they depend on and encourage the system to manage them medically. They follow doctors' orders and pay bills promptly.

Likely to be covered by employer-provided standard health insurance, traditional health care consumers "abdicate responsibility for their own health." They choose a hospital and doctor using recommendations from friends, and convenience. Only 30 percent would switch doctors even if they could save on their insurance premiums.

■ **Modern health care consumers** are oriented towards wellness, prevention and education. Most have yet to develop chronic conditions and, except for chemical dependency and mental problems, are relatively disease-free. With fewer loyalties and a more skeptical attitude about the benefits of physician care and hospitalization, they are causing a dramatic shift in health care settings. The more formalized inpatient setting is giving way to speedier outpatient care. They are the major customers of minor emergency centers, surgicenters and other freestanding clinics.

Modern health care consumers are cost-oriented and shop around, displaying a willingness to switch. Less likely to have a family doctor than older consumers, they want to be part of the health care process. "They are more concerned with personal control than security. The women in this group are economically and socially independent."

■ **Should you choose one market over another?** Thomas and Sehnert acknowledge that a dual health care market complicates product mix and service delivery for health care providers, but caution that "focusing on either the traditionals or the modern may unnecessarily limit the customer base. Health care providers that offer specialized services, such as women's health care, may want to approach both the traditional and modern markets, but with different techniques."

And it appears unlikely that modern consumers will become more traditional with age, as their characteristics are rooted in their past experiences. Eventually, the dual health care market will be replaced by the modern market. This chapter will suggest marketing keys to help you during the 1990s—the key transition period.

THE PROGNOSIS FOR HEALTH CARE PRODUCTS AND SERVICES

Challenges for delivering traditional physician and health care services abound. With the American population both rapidly aging and living longer, traditional physician and hospital health care services will continue to dominate the health care business. However, there have been, and will continue to be, dramatic changes in who delivers these services, and how and where the services are provided.

■ **The day of the individual practitioner is passing.** As the traditional health care market gives way to the modern health care market, physicians are delivering their services differently:

- **By the year 2000, most Americans will belong to an HMO (health maintenance organization) or other fixed-fee medical plan,** receiving comprehensive care for a flat fee. In 1989, for the first time, more doctors were employees than were self-employed, according to the American Medical Association.

- **Specialization, rather than primary care, has been the trend,** due in large part to the health insurance reimbursement policies, which pay larger fees for operations and procedures, and smaller fees for primary-care and preventional medicine.

- **Medicine is heading towards a demographic revolution** as women and minorities replace the traditional white male dominance. Women, for example, are often more interested in the specialties that treat the primary medical needs of patients. They also have lower income expectations than highly paid specialties like surgery.

■ **Most operations will be performed in doctors' offices or small "surgi-clinics,"** a trend fueled in large part by government and private industry attempting to slow spiraling health costs.

THE MODERN HEALTH CARE MARKET

■ **The preventative health care market is booming, thanks to boomers.** The American "Quest for Youth" or diet market is already a $32.4 billion industry, and is expected to grow to $50.7 billion by 1995. According to Jeff Ostroff, author of *Successful Marketing to the 50+ Consumer,* "Spanish explorer Ponce de Leon would have felt right at home if he had lived in the United States at the beginning of the 21st century. For never before in this country's history will so many Americans over 45 be striving to **regain** or **retain** a youthful appearance and attitude."

In 1988 alone, according to a study by Marketdata Enterprises, Americans cheerfully spent:

Total Dollars (billions)	Products
10.0	Diet soft drinks
4.5	Hospital-sponsored weight loss programs
8.0	Health spas and exercise clubs
2.5	Low-calorie foods
1.5	Weight-loss clinics and programs
1.4	Resort spas
10.4	Diet books and cassettes
.3	Appetite suppressants

Ostroff asserts there are three things that will be responsible for mature America's obsession with trying to look and feel young:

- **There will be an overwhelming supply of evidence to support the notion that older adults can indeed retard or even reverse some of the declines typically associated with aging.** Perhaps the greatest testament of this will be the giant army of older role models who will irrefutably bear witness to the remarkable possibilities offered by healthy lifestyles, breakthroughs in aging research, and improved medical products, treatments, and technologies.

- **America's major health care purchasers will also stimulate the move to keep a graying America young.** Faced with the enormous burden of paying medical costs to support the older population, government programs, large and mid-size employers, and union trust fund managers will do everything possible to continue the wellness movement of the 1980s and early 1990s. As part of this effort, all kinds of incentives (financial and other) will be offered to encourage the practice of preventive medicine.

- **No force will have a greater impact on the quest for the fountain of youth than the aging of the baby boomers.** Having built their identity as America's youth generation, the boomers will not enter the second half of life with a whimper. Instead, they'll do everything they can to delay or counteract the effects of aging. And, in the process, they'll create the biggest market the health and fitness industry has ever known.

■ **Areas of opportunity abound in the health and fitness market.** The people most likely to take action to improve their health are those in the middle-years, age 35 to 59, according to *Prevention* magazine. Faced with their own mortality, they are trying to fight back. And these are also the people most likely to buy and use health-oriented products.

Ostroff highlights a number of products and services he believes will do well with modern health care consumers:

- exercise, fitness, and weight-reducing centers

- exercise and athletic equipment

- cosmetic surgery

- wellness-oriented publications and software packages

- exercise videotapes

- rehabilitation services (such as sports medicine)

- vitamins

- fitness and "rebirthing" vacations and camps (i.e., where one's psyche is uplifted or rejuvenated)

- "anti-aging" personal care products (sunscreens, "anti-wrinkle" creams, skin moisturizers, and hair colorings)

- healthful foods, such as fruits, vegetables, pasta, whole-grain breads and cereals, fish, poultry, and the *low* products (low fat, low calorie, low salt, low sugar, low cholesterol, etc.)

- sports participation

- self-testing programs and products (health screenings and kits/equipment which check blood-sugar levels, blood pressure, or cholesterol)

- drugs and devices which combat or mask declines in health (cholesterol or sugar-lowering drugs, bifocal contact lenses, "invisible" hearing aids, etc.)

- healthful food stores and restaurants

MARKETING STRATEGIES FOR HEALTH CARE PRODUCTS AND SERVICES

■ **Increased competition has lead to aggressive marketing tactics.** The number of physicians in the United States today is nearly double that of 1965: 486,000 versus 298,000. While referrals are still the primary source of patients, health providers are increasingly marketing for patients. Many health maintenance organizations do extensive telephone and mail solicitation of the elderly, sometimes spending 20 percent of their budgets on advertising and promotion.

"During the 1980s, hospitals learned how to target
segments and niches with relevant advertising. They
are rising to the challenge of learning how to maxi-
mize interaction with each of the targeted groups
they want to attract. Substance abuse treatment programs, senior citizen clubs, maternity centers and
diet plans are a few of the 'products' now being pro-
moted heavily with direct response mail and phone
advertising," notes Stan Rapp, co-founder of Rapp &
Collins, a leading direct marketing agency.

Many hospitals and physicians now use a regular schedule of acquisition mailings. Providence Milwaukie Hospital in
Portland, Oregon, does an end-of-year mailing wishing selected audiences "healthy, happy holidays." In addition to
serving as a schedule of their extensive community education
health services and classes, the mailing suggests "giving your
special someone a gift of knowledge, with a health education
class from Providence Milwaukie Hospital" and offers to send
a gift certificate to that special someone.

■ **Your best target, demographically, is older Americans.** Many
American hospitals and health care providers are finally facing the reality that people over the age of 55 now account for
more than 50 percent of health care costs. By the year 2000,
when the baby boomer population joins the older American
population, that figure is expected to rise above 70 percent.

At the 468-bed nonprofit El Camino hospital, which
serves much of four Silicon Valley communities south of San
Francisco, recognition of the need to cultivate older Americans
resulted in the printing of an orientation leaflet in boldface
type large enough for all eyes to read.

In addition, El Camino has retrained its staff in the needs
and sensitivities of older patients; altered its menus to provide
smaller, more frequent meals attuned to older appetites; extended visiting hours to allow working adult children more
time with their hospitalized parents; and set up counselling
services to help patients through the Medicare maze, or with
choosing a nursing-care facility.

El Camino's changes extend beyond the hospital and into
the homes of the patients themselves. "We recognize that

health care isn't limited to the period of hospitalization," says Neilson Buchanan, El Camino's president and chief executive officer. "It includes what happens before, during and after."

When a patient over the age of 65 is ready to leave El Camino, Project Transition takes over. If necessary, a volunteer is assigned to escort the patient home, get him/her settled, and follow up for a week.

Another program, Advantage 65, gives members discounts at pharmacies, opticians, hearing centers, nursing services, and even restaurants and theaters.

■ **Baby Boomers are, increasingly, a "sandwiched" generation.** Many, especially women, are balancing health concerns for themselves and children with emerging care needs of parents.

● **Respond to the boomers' needs to take charge of their health care decisions.** The Prologue patient referral system is a high-tech telecommunications system that provides each caller a chance to choose the right doctor. Consumers dial a toll-free number to speak to a specially trained Prologue counselor who matches the caller's medical needs to the best qualified physician in the Prologue database.

Each physician in the network has completed an extensive survey with 1,300 coded information variables. Health care consumers/customers looking for a doctor can check treatment manner, credentials, convenience, accessibility and personal characteristics before visiting the office. By early 1989, Prologue had already provided 2 million callers with information and scheduled 500,000 appointments, with a 95 percent satisfaction rate.

● **Provide information on areas of concern.** Because modern health care consumers/customers take responsibility for their own health care decisions, they welcome information. St. Mary's Hospital Medical center in Green Bay, Wisconsin, used their own Pagemaker software to publish the book, *Pregnancy, A Time for Caring*. It is the centerpiece of St. Mary's marketing effort for its obstetrical services, and is used to attract referrals for their specialists at the birthing center. Notes Stan Rapp,

''There is a striking parallel between their use of the book to build a relationship with expectant parents and the Huggies mailings of educational material to build loyalty for their brand of diapers.''

● **Offer some services as 'loss leaders.'** A doctor in Richfield, Connecticut, mailed 20,000 letters offering a cholesterol test for $5 and a school physical exam for children for $15. It was an introductory offer to bring patients into the newly established office. The letter was professionally written and set just the right tone for a physician. The result was several thousand responses that are estimated to represent $500,000 in patient services.

● **Find a niche.** *AIDS Patient Care* is one of the first trade publications detailing research in AIDS. While readers are mainly health professionals, families and patients also receive the magazine. (AIDS will cost the United States more than $37 billion between 1986 and 1991, or 1 percent of all U.S. health spending.)

In New Jersey, surgeons Dr. Ira Rutkow and Dr. Alan W. Robbins operate the Hernia Center (dial 1-800-HERNIAS), offering all-inclusive hernia operation packages. Rutkow says their high volume and specialization allows them to deliver good care at a better cost.

Eldercare, especially for Alzheimer's sufferers, may be the health care niche of the future. A new study in the *Journal of the American Medical Association* finds that 47 percent of people who live to age 85 have Alzheimer's disease. Three percent of those between ages 65 and 74 are already affected, as are 18.7 percent of those 75 to 84 years old. The over-85 age group is already the fastest-growing segment of the U.S. population, and cases of Alzheimer's disease will increase along with the number of octogenarians. When the baby boom reaches its 80s, 14 million of them could have Alzheimer's.

For every affected person, an average of three other victims —already 12 million people, experts figure—are heavily burdened with the financial and caregiving problems this disease brings.

The demand for elder-care is growing. As millions of middle-aged women have been forced to give up jobs, employers are feeling the toll as well. Some companies are beginning to realize they may need to provide elder-care as one of their benefits, if they are to retain valued employees.

■ **Women are the primary health care decision-makers.** "I've seen data that say women make 80 percent of the health decisions," notes Bernard Kingsley, marketing director for Durham County General Hospital.

● **Target women moving into your area.** Kingsley set out to market programs to key demographic groups. Durham County General Hospital promotes to women using demographic information from private companies, the state, and county planners. You can too. And use welcome wagon and other relocation services, or arrange with the local school(s) to provide emergency cards, poison control information, etc. to recently arrived households. Consider offering tours of your facility or a special "get-acquainted" workshop targeted to the women's role as the health care decision-maker.

● **Use targeted media advertising.** The Headache Treatment Center runs a direct response campaign in women's magazines that develops hundreds of qualified prospects. Working with Greenwich Hospital, they devised a special unit for treatment. Advertising runs in regional editions of national publications, and is building an invaluable database. More than 10 percent of headache sufferers who come to a doctor's office are admitted to a hospital for treatment of their symptoms.

■ **Target to minorities,** both native and immigrating populations. Health care is one of life's basic necessities.

● **Minorities are often newcomers.** Kingsley is also sensitive to attracting newcomers from foreign countries, another large target for Durham County. Durham's Physician Locator pamphlet profiles local doctors, including information on everything from where they got their degree to whether they speak a foreign language.

With the increasing Hispanic-American population, most health and hospital facilities should consider printing a guide in Spanish, and marketing regularly through Hispanic media and publications. In some areas of the United States, publications in Japanese, Vietnamese, Laotian, and Chinese are also useful.

● **Lower-income households are good markets.** A point to note, with minorities often heavily represented in lower income groups. New data from the Bureau of Labor Statistics shows that the poor spend as much as the affluent on health care, *if household size is taken into account.* The average high-income household has 3.2 people, compared with 2 in the average low-income household.

■ **Marry psychographics to demographics to identify "lifestyle" target groups for health care products and services.** *The Fit & The Fat, A Prevention Report on Patterns in Health Behavior* identifies six lifestyle segments based on health and safety behavior.

The analysis, conducted by Louis Harris & Associates, defines clusters of people who differ from one another in health and safety behavior, and has developed groups that are both distinct and coherent:

- The Healthy and Wealthy

- The Safe and Satisfied

- The Sedentary but Striving

- The Young and Reckless

- The Fat and Frustrated

- The Confused and Indifferent

● **The Healthy and Wealthy,** despite some weaknesses, rate at the top in overall health behavior and want to do better. They represent 25 percent of the population and have the best habits. They get check-ups, watch their diets, and wear seat belts. They are also most likely to buy healthy food, which is low-fat and high-fiber. Interestingly, while they are the most likely group to walk for fitness, they rate below the national average for more strenuous exercise.

Demographically, of these 45 million people, 56 percent are female. They have a middle-aged skew (45 percent are 35 to 59, compared to 38 percent for the U.S. population). Compared to the country as a whole, they are more likely to have a college or graduate degree, a high household income, and a job as a professional or manager.

● **The Safe and Satisfied** have fairly healthy lifestyles, and they seem content with their level of effort. They represent seven percent of the population. They are tied for last in willingness to spend money on things that are healthy, and the least likely to buy health-oriented food products. However, they have the best record for an annual cholesterol test, and 62 percent get regular strenuous exercise, compared to just 36 percent for the U.S.

Demographically, these 13 million Americans are almost equally divided between men and women. Forty-two percent are over 50, compared to 35 percent for the U.S. They are slightly below average for education levels and household income, with a high percentage of unskilled workers.

● **The Sedentary but Striving** are slightly above average in health behavior, but are eager to improve. They represent 8 percent of the population. Seventy-seven percent are overweight, but this group has the highest percentage of individuals who want to exercise, eat better, and gain self-control. They are below average, however, in willingness to spend extra money for things that are healthy, perhaps because of income constraints.

Demographically, nearly two-thirds of these 14.5 million Americans are women. They are older than the U.S. average, with about one-third falling into the 18 to 34 group, another third in the 35 to 59 group, and the remaining third 60 + . They are more likely to be minorities—21 percent black versus 12 percent for the U.S.; 8 percent Hispanic versus 6 percent for the U.S., and have the lowest income level and a high percentage of blue-collar workers.

● **The Young and Reckless,** the largest of the groups at 38 percent, know a lot about health habits but are often unwilling to act on their knowledge. These 68 million Americans do well at getting frequent strenuous exercise (eight points above the national average of 36 percent), but are least likely to believe that health clubs are important for physical fitness. It's very important for them to feel that they are attractive to the opposite sex.

Demographically, males have a slight (51 percent) majority, are younger than average (48 percent under 35, compared to 39 percent of the U.S.), and are slightly above average for education level and household income. Their racial make-up and job levels match the U.S. average fairly closely.

● **The Fat and Frustrated** have a strong desire to be healthy, but lack the resources and knowledge necessary for success. Eight percent of the U.S. population, they have the highest percentage who are trying to lose weight, but the lowest percentage who have been successful at keeping weight off. They rarely exercise, but are the most likely to buy diet books and non-prescription diet pills. And they purchase low-calorie and low-fat/low-cholesterol foods at higher than average rates.

Demographically, the 13 million people in this group are predominantly female (57 percent) and somewhat older than average. About one-third are over 50, compared to 23 percent for the U.S.; nearly half are age 35 to 59, compared to 38 percent for the U.S. They are more likely to be minorities, and they have the lowest education level of any group.

● **The Confused and Indifferent,** as might be expected, rank lowest in health behavior, and don't seem to care. They represent five percent of the population. They are not a particularly good audience for any health-related products or services.

Demographically, men are a slight majority (53 percent) in this 9 million member group. They are predominantly white, and have slightly lower than average education and income levels. They are scattered about evenly among all age groups and are most likely to work at blue collar jobs.

Of all the business markets you could choose, health care products and services probably represent the greatest opportunity as we move through the 1990s and into the twenty-first century. According to Wendy Gray, benefits specialist at The Conference Board, the federal budget for 2005 is expected to include more spending for Medicare than for Social Security or defense. Add that to private and company spending, and no other area comes close in dollar spending. The national preoccupation with health can lead to your wealth.

CHAPTER FOURTEEN

Making Pleasure a Profitable Business: Leisure and Travel

THE FASTEST GROWING business may be pleasure. Recreation has become the fifth biggest category of personal consumption expenditures, surpassing spending on clothing in 1987.

American Demographics reports that recreation is hot on the heels of other major expenditure categories. At $247 billion in 1988, spending on recreation has grown to more than half of spending on transportation ($4.06 billion) or medical care ($443 billion). It's approaching half of spending on food ($597 billion), and one-third of spending on housing ($887 billion).

■ **Overall, the most rapidly growing single category of recreation spending is "commercial participant amusements," rising from $2.4 billion in 1970 to $18.9 billion in 1988.** What falls in this category? Products and services associated with active activities: fees for playing tennis, attending golf tournaments, vacations at Disney World, or a fitness spa are examples.

These participatory amusements ranked seventh among categories of recreation spending in 1970. By 1988, they had moved into fourth place—behind only video and audio equipment, toys, and sports equipment—and far surpassing spending on spectator events.

What's triggering this growth? A combination of demographic, socioeconomic, and psychographic factors including:

- **The baby boomers' adoption of a more cyclic lifestyle** (described in Chapter 12). Many are taking retirement in chunks, as they pursue careers and continuing education, expanding the market for "mini" vacations and short-duration leisure activities. Of special interest: activities which provide spiritual, educational, and social fulfillment.

- **The growth of the mature market of individuals with more income, better health, and higher levels of education.** As the nest empties, vacation time accumulates, and retirement beckons, older Americans will increase the demand for lengthier vacations such as cruises with exotic destinations, and extended weekend activities.

- **The growth of large numbers of mature "singles" (whether divorced, widowed, or never married). Heavily female,** they will seek out companionship programs and services both for vacations, and shorter leisure time activities.

- **The return of the family, both through the boomer "boomlet" and increasing numbers of middle-class minority families,** is fueling a return to multi-generational leisure and recreational pastimes.

It's hard to think of a recreational/leisure business, whether participatory or spectator, which *couldn't* benefit in the years ahead. The audiences—with the money and time— are available for restaurants, hotels, airlines, theme parks, cruise liners, recreational vehicle and luxury car/van manufacturers, resorts, sports and fitness camps, events and performances, tour organizers, and those that interface with these groups (food and beverage suppliers, cultural attractions, sports equipment manufacturers, and the entertainment industry).

But to live up to their potential, leisure activity businesses will need to know their audiences—boomers, aging Americans, working women, and minorities.

MARKETING PARTICIPATORY LEISURE ACTIVITIES—TRAVEL

The number of consumers who stay overnight at either a hotel or motel each month continues to climb. In a typical month, according to *The Public Pulse*, 36 million consumers —one in five Americans—visited a hotel or motel at least once.

And, although business travel is also on the rise, most of these consumers are traveling for pleasure. Nineteen percent travelled 200 miles or more on a vacation trip, compared to 9 percent who made a business trip of a similar length. Only executives and professionals are just as likely to take business trips as vacation journeys: 24 percent travel for pleasure and 23 percent travel for business during a typical month.

Who travels? All of our key demographic groups are good prospects for businesses catering to the leisure travel market. Here are some of the marketing keys to consider.

■ **Boomers especially will be drawn towards leisure activities which enhance their well-being, or provide them with new or meaningful experiences.** According to Jeff Ostroff, because this group has a higher level of education and worldly experience than previous generations, they will want to know the "why" and "how" behind what they learn or see, along with the "what," "where," and "when."

In leisure travel, this suggests a booming market for adventure or fitness-oriented travel (visits to offbeat locations, mystery tours, scientific expeditions, and tennis and spa vacations) as well as combination travel/education packages.

One leisure travel-oriented company which has successfully target-marketed to boomers is Club Med. Originally positioned as the "get-away, do it all" retreat for single, young baby boomers, Club Med has carefully changed its positioning as the boomers have matured. In the 1990s, the Clubs are focusing on new markets, adding mainstream features, and more intensive fitness programs to their famed laid-back lifestyle. Today, the villages welcome company training seminars, professional golf and other sports tournaments, and families (with 38 Mini and 13 Baby Clubs catering to children ages 11 years down to 4 months old). And, responding to the demand for shorter vacations, Club Med has even modified its one-week-only vacation packages to provide long weekends and miniweeks.

■ **Heavily driven by both the baby boomers and older Americans, the trend is towards shorter but more frequent vacations.** According to *Research Alert*, Americans want to "Hit the road more often, but get home faster." For their summer vacations, for example, 32 percent of all adults are planning trips of less than two weeks (up from 27 percent in 1974), while 18 percent will be taking trips of two weeks or more (down from 26 percent). The popularity of weekend travel (up 41 percent just since 1982), moreover, seems bound to increase.

Most popular? Trips for entertainment and outdoor recreation (9.6 percent) and vacation trips as a whole (8.4 percent) rose more than twice as fast as the overall increase in travel (4.2 percent). But trips to visit friends and relatives declined for the second straight year (down by 2.5 percent). By far the most popular place to vacation is the South Atlantic region, attracting over one-fifth of all U.S. trips during 1988. The least popular region was New England, comprising less that 4 percent of all U.S. person-trips for that year.

■ **Cruises are making waves.** Only 4 to 5 percent of Americans have ever been on a cruise. Yet growth has been phenomenal: the short cruise (3 to 5 days) has grown over 200 percent in the past decade, while the week-long cruise (6 to 8 days) has grown 100 percent. And cruise-takers are extremely loyal: 85 percent are repeaters.

The future looks even brighter, with Bob Dickinson, senior vice president for marketing and sales for Carnival Cruise Line, predicting that 10 million passengers will be cruising by the year 2000. He has good reason for such optimism. Almost three-quarters (74 percent) of adult households with annual incomes of $25,000 or more who haven't yet cruised indicate it's a vacation they plan to take in the future.

Mel Gordon, owner of the World Cruise Center in Portland, Oregon, agrees. He says: "We're looking at a 95 percent target market. Baby boomers are entering midlife, the kids are grown and gone, and they have a lot more spendable income."

Other opportunities: mature Americans' interest in lengthier vacations coupled with the convenience of a cruise's all-inclusiveness; singles-oriented cruises; and multi-generational cruises.

■ **Family vacations, heavily boomer driven, represented 59 percent of the vacation travel market in 1988,** up 21 percent since 1983. Families are more likely than the average traveler to go by car and less likely to fly (15 percent versus 24 percent for the average traveler).

Many boomers seem determined to give their young children the experiences they dreamed about in the 1950s. Travel to theme parks, Club Meds, and trips outside the U.S. are all experiencing a family boom.

■ **Bus and rail travel, heavily used by less affluent travelers, is growing strongly.** Greyhound, for example, after suffering a 45 percent decline in passenger miles from 1980 to 1986, is enjoying its third straight year of strong recovery. 1989 was the second year in a row that Greyhound's growth outpaced that of air, auto, and rail travel. Demographically, the future appears strong, as minorities and the elderly are well-represented in the 70 percent of their passengers who live in under-$20,000/year households. But a caution: A significant number of new bus riders traditionally come from the young adult age groups, which are decreasing in population.

MARKETING PARTICIPATORY LEISURE ACTIVITIES—SPORTS AND HOBBIES

■ **Americans love their sports and hobbies!** Catering to the needs of enthusiastic participants can be a profitable business if you respond to demographic trends.

● **Bowling** is making a comeback, after being hit by changing demographics of the workplace and America's changing ideas of leisure, reports *American Demographics*.

In the 1960s and early 1970s, everyone bowled. Not only was it a family activity—often the only game in town—but it was part of fabric of the work mode. Men and women who worked together bowled together.

In the mid-1970s, 60 to 70 percent of the nation's bowling leagues were tied to private organizations such as companies. Today, only 30 percent are tied to organizations. Bowling proprietors are now organizing leagues themselves. This is according to Charles Martin, marketing professor at Wichita State University, Kansas, and a bowling industry expert.

And when company bowling leagues took a break for the summer, women's daytime leagues kept the revenue coming in. But the entry of women into the work force and the increased number of leisure-time options available added two more blows to the bowling industry. [Those who would be] today's bowlers divide their time between home videos and racquetball. Few are willing (or able) to make the time commitment that league bowling traditionally requires; once a week for as many as 35 weeks a year.

Bowling proprietors use targeted marketing to promote this American pastime. Making bowling attractive to the baby boom family, says Lance Elliot, executive director of the National Bowling Council in Washington, D.C., means offering quality service and appealing facilities. Glossy mega-lane "bowling recreation centers" with computerized scoring, cocktail lounges, and daycare services are replacing the old neighborhood bowling alley.

For the serious upscale bowler, equipment manufacturers like Brunswick offer precision-balanced bowling balls and instant-replay video displays that allow players to review their delivery of the ball. And for the health-conscious, some lanes advertise "bowl-aerobics," offering two games of bowling followed by one hour of aerobics.

Bowling center operators now use target marketing techniques, says Elliot. Telemarketing and direct mail reach league dropouts and entice the casual bowler to return more often. In addition to introducing bowling into school programs, proprietors are using promotion videos like "The Perfect Game" to target older bowlers.

There are signs that bowlings' marketing efforts are paying off. Non-league bowling, including casual play and organized activities (such as bowling at children's birthday parties) grew by 5.8 percent for the year ending in February 1989, says Charles Martin. Senior league play grew 6.5 percent. Of all the new bowlers, older Americans who live an active lifestyle have become the most dedicated players. "We do it for fun and friendship," says Vilma Galitza, an AARP member who helped organize Friday-afternoon senior leagues at Suburban Lanes in Bucyrus, Ohio. "We have one gentleman who is 82 and an excellent bowler, and several people in their 70s," she says. "They yell just like any teenager when they get a strike."

Different sports and hobbies appeal to individuals with varying demographics and psychographics. Here are some highlights to consider:

■ Over a third (35 percent) of U.S. households enjoy **gardening**. Gardeners tend to be older than average (median age is 51), are married, with a median household income of $28,930. Interestingly, there is a growing representation of gardeners in affluent households.

Other activities gardeners enjoy: furnishing/decorating, home workshops, sewing, and wildlife/environmentalism.

■ Almost a quarter (23 percent) of American households enjoy **photography**. While the median age of household heads in shutter-happy homes is 41, you'll find greater numbers of younger Americans than in the general population. Males, and families without kids, are overrepresented, as are households with incomes over $75,000.

Other interests include: electronics, science fiction, foreign travel, wildlife/environmentalism, and wines.

■ Twenty-four percent of Americans, heavily older, single and female with a median age of 47 years, consider **catalog shopping** a hobby. They show a greater interest than the general public in fashion clothing, entering sweepstakes, and health foods/vitamins.

■ Fifteen percent of U.S. households share an interest in **wildlife/environmentalism**. The median age of the household is 43, yet wildlife/environmentalist households tend to be headed by younger people. Single males are overrepresented, and these households have more interest than the general public in science/new technology, science fiction, hunting/shooting, and fine arts/antiques.

■ Ten percent of the U.S. population are **golfers**. Overwhelmingly male (78 percent), they are a relatively affluent and educated set. The greatest percentage of golfers (23 percent) resides in the East North Central region of the U.S.

■ **Boomers**, generally, are a good market for activities which provide "hands-on" participation or offer "inside" information (e.g., winemaking, filmmaking, and farm and factory tours) as well as for special interest tours and courses, says Jeff Ostroff.

MARKETING PARTICIPATORY LEISURE ACTIVITIES—EATING OUT AND IN

■ **"Let's eat out" was the rallying cry of the 1980s, but a slowdown is predicted for the 1990s.** Several demographic and psychographic factors figure in the predictions for lean times ahead.

● **The general slowing in the rate of women joining the work force is considered a key.** While women still continue to enter the labor market, the percentage and number gains are proportionately much less than in the 1980s.

● **Baby boomers have shifted away from fast food** and towards higher-quality restaurants with more ambiance and healthier foods. The smaller baby buster market is also impacting on the fast food market. Good news? Older Americans on modest pensions and many of our lower income minorities continue to patronize these restaurants.

● **Moderately priced family sit-down restaurants are showing growth in an otherwise flat industry.** Per-store sales have increased about 5 to 6 percent annually in recent years, and the segment has room to grow.

The hottest food trend for restaurants for the next few years is expected to be the expansion of Italian sit-down dining establishments. These imitate the success of General Mills' Olive Garden, which was voted the No. 1 dinner house of 1989 in a consumer poll conducted by *Restaurants and Institutions*. Chili's Inc., often cited as the star of sit-down restaurants, is opening a competing chain, Macaroni Grills, across the country.

● **Many families and two-career couples find eating out too much of a hassle.** The microwave has made even fast food seem slow. Take-outs—at all price levels—are growing. Some restaurants now put drive-through windows on two sides of their buildings. It has proven to be a popular move with the working class.

Convenience isn't all at the low end of the scale. Restaurant Express of Newport Beach, California, delivers as many as 1,000 dishes a week, mostly from white-tablecloth restaurants in southern California. For a $4 charge, drivers in tuxedos will deliver meals from more than 30 restaurants, be it a filet mignon from Newport Beach's Villa Nova or a poached salmon with black truffles from Le Midi.

● **Target unusual food to boomers and the "young elderly."** People age 30 to 59 are more adventurous in their eating habits than are older or younger consumers. Whether it's ethnic or exotic, upscale or just uncooked—the middle-aged are more apt to try it.

Marketing Spectator Leisure Activities

■ **The ultimate spectator business may well be supplying owners of VCRs with an endless supply of entertaining (and educational) tapes.** How good an audience is there? Consider these 1989 facts:

- Ninety-one percent of consumers with annual incomes greater than $50,000 now own a VCR.

- Among consumers earning between $25,000 and $50,000 per year, VCR ownership has reached 78 percent.

- Nationally, 61 percent of the population now owns a VCR—up sharply from 48 percent in 1988, and nearly three times as many as in 1986.

Looking at our key demographic groups, we also find that:

- Boomers are heavy users of VCRs. Seventy-eight percent of those age 30 to 44, and 77 percent of parents of children under 18 years of age have VCR machines. Households renting at least twenty-four videotapes a year are likely to be headed by 35- to 44-year-olds who have attended college, and include children age 6 to 18.

- Sixty-six percent of Hispanic Americans own VCRs.

Jeff Ostroff suggests there will be a strong market for videocassette travelogues, which allow older Americans to visit places without ever leaving their front door.

The growing interest in lifelong learning suggests that sponsored programs by hospitals, banks, and universities will find their niche as well.

And Louis Harris and Associates suggest* that the VCR may "revolutionize funding for the arts overnight" as, **increasingly, Americans will use VCRs to counter lack of leisure time**. Many Americans enjoy spectator activities, whether it's a sports tournament, a fine arts show, or an entertainment performance, but, increasingly, busy people don't have time to attend the actual event. While the number of people going to live presentations appears to be entering a period of slow absolute decline,

> more than three-quarters of all VCR owners (42 percent of all adults) say it is certain or probable they would buy or rent videocassettes of hit musical comedies and musical theater shows. Almost two-thirds would be in the market for videocassettes of new hit plays on Broadway and in London. Over half said they are interested in buying or renting videocassettes of the best pop concerts just after they have taken place. People also expressed a desire to buy or rent videocassettes of symphony concerts, art exhibits, and even opera, notes the Harris report.

---

*In America and the Arts V, a study done for Phillip Morris.

Marketing Keys for Spectator Events

■ **The performing and fine arts always struggle to attract the public's attention.** Only 4 to 12 percent of the total U.S. population visit museums and art exhibits or attend live performances of the opera, symphony, and dance.

In many ways, the next ten to twenty years are transitional ones for fine and performing arts organizations:

● **Recognize it's a changing market.** The typical arts attendee has tended to fit a demographic pattern of being white, female, happily married or widowed, older, affluent and Protestant. Psychographically, they have tended to be Outer-Directed Achievers. This is a shrinking market with intense competition.

Psychographically, attendees of performing and fine arts events in the 1990s are more likely to be Inner-Directed. While large numbers of Outer-Directed Achievers enjoy the arts, the entire range of Inner-Directed persons—from the younger I-Am-Me's to the heavily female Experientials to the boomer-laden Societally Conscious—display interest in fine and performing arts. With our society shifting towards Inner-Directedness, this provides good opportunities for the marketer. (Review Chapter 3.)

● **First and foremost, strengthen your ties with current attendees.** Arts organizations cannot afford to lose current supporters because of indifferent cultivation. Often attendees are not aware of how fragile the financial base of their favorite arts organization is. Communicate openly to your supporters and back up the information with demonstrations of appreciation to those who buy subscriptions or multiple tickets. For example, Achievers like recognition, and respond well to ''members only'' events, a chance to meet the artist, and ''perks'' like valet parking.

● **Look at the major societal trends to find niches to work more strongly.** A word of caution: often, arts organizations appear unfriendly to new attendees. All the groups profiled need messages that they will be treated as special by the arts organization they support.

Because *baby boomers* combine work and leisure, often looking for networking opportunities, the upscale image of arts events could be an attraction. "It's entertaining, and it's good for business," notes Mimi Johnson, vice president of Stephen Dunn & Associates, a Los Angeles-based marketing and fund raising firm specializing in phone campaigns for arts organizations. "Spending an evening at the opera, symphony, or ballet can make a good impression on the business contact you might bump into in the lobby."

Consider backing a performance with a fund raising special event. The glamour, the opportunity to dress up, the upscale tickets all reinforce the boomer's sense of being unique. Be sure to follow the cardinal rule if you want to attract baby boomers: keep them moving. Remember, boomers attend your events for both business and social reasons. They can't mix freely if your event requires them to stay in place, at one table or without conversation, all the time.

And make use of nostalgia. Whether it's movie or music, baby boomers hark back to the 1950s and 1960s. One reason for the nostalgia boom: today's parents want to share their past with their children. It's becoming common to see parents and children cheering stars of the 1960s and 1970s at concerts.

But it doesn't end there. Halloween, for example, has become a big business. "It's no longer a children's holiday. The majority of dollars are spent on adults," says Jack Sheehan, owner of the Costumer in upstate New York. Fifty million adults attended Halloween parties in 1988, an increase of 25 percent over the previous three years. It's the second-largest adult party-giving occasion in the United States, following only New Year's Eve in popularity.

Hispanic-Americans have been ignored by many arts organizations. Yet entertainers like Madonna, Sting, Michael Jackson, Linda Ronstadt, and Julio Iglesias have all released records with lyrics in Spanish, which have proved best sellers both with their traditional audiences and with Hispanic buyers. "Right now you are looking at a Latin population in America that is proportionate to what the black population was when Motown took off," says New York-based musician and producer Jellybean Benitez. "You're looking at Latins who have already assimilated into the culture and have discretionary incomes. And they are purchasing records."

In fact, Hispanic-Americans have a rich heritage of appreciation of the arts. Whether it is paintings, music, or dance, Hispanic culture is "consumed with the past, on both the personal and historical levels, and drawn to the memory play, the history painting, the musical tradition to accomplish the tasks of recollection," raved Time in an issue featuring Hispanic-American cultural contributions.

As Hispanic-Americans continue to gain economically, their loyalty and Outer-Directedness makes them prime prospects for arts organizations. Currently, this is a largely untapped market. Because Hispanic-Americans value family and community interaction above all, demonstrations that indicate their participation is desired will act as a signal to large numbers of individuals.

Welcoming gestures are called for. Including Hispanic-American cultural vehicles in an arts organization's season or programs can be sensitively done. (Organizations have learned tact. In the late 1960s, the Metropolitan Museum of Art in New York City confidently declared that spending $5,544,000 on Velazquez's portrait of Juan de Pareja, his dark-skinned assistant of presumed Moorish ancestry, would improve the self-esteem of the museum's black and Hispanic public. It didn't.)

Having docents, tour guides, and ushers who are bilingual in English and Spanish, and offering subscription brochures, programs, and other written materials in a bilingual format sends a message of inclusion.

The "young" older American is a prime target for arts and entertainment organizations looking for new audiences. Between 1990 and the year 2000, the number of prime-lifers, those age 50 to 64, will grow by 25 percent as baby boomers begin to infiltrate that age group.

Older Americans both enjoy being at home and want to get away. The arts can satisfy both longings. Attract more mature audiences with brochures and programs that take into account vision problems by using larger and bolder type. Entice individuals by scheduling events at times and locations that appeal to them. Many don't like driving at night: Either test afternoon and weekend events or provide transportation. Look at your facility with an "older" eye: Is is barrier-free? Well-lighted? Don't forget to test sound and lighting systems. Then, package videocassettes or tapes that allow the armchair tourist to enjoy cultural events at home.

Recognize that many "younger" older Americans travel extensively. Explore exchanging lists with like-organizations in other cities and states. Extend discounted memberships for short-term stays and last minute ticket buyers.

Remember that rising divorce rates and increasing late-life widowhood in the past two decades have led to an increase of 123 percent in the number of older people living alone—over two and a half times the growth rate of the older population in general. In fact, of the total population of older Americans, 43 percent are single. Arts and cultural organizations can offer unattached individuals an opportunity to participate in opening nights, preview exhibits and "VIP" viewings; glittering special events where the lack of a partner is not a problem.

Consider giving older Americans a "test drive." *Modern Maturity* suggests, in a series on how to attract mature America, that you should "let them get behind the wheel. Give them a trial period. A sample. A coupon. Americans over 50 are more likely than others to consider purchases carefully. With the experience of maturity, they analyze in order to buy wisely. They'd like a taste of the pie before they splurge on the whole thing. And they'll want to know about your refund policy, your guarantees and warranties. Don't be afraid to give details. In return, over-50 will buy, knowing what they're getting. You'll fulfill expectations. They'll be satisfied. Loyal. They'll be back for more." Your "give-away" in the form of a free ticket is a smart investment in a key market.

Segment *working women* into married working woman (with and without children), and single women for most effective targeting.

Unlike the older American target population, finding ways to fill time is not a concern for the married working woman. Often she is juggling multiple roles, and trying to plan leisure and educational activities for children, spouse, and self. Two-income couples with children make up more than 40 percent of all couples in the childbearing ages. It makes sense for arts organizations to consider marketing strategies that appeal to the women—typically the decision-maker for family entertainment.

Working women with children tend to be baby boomers, between ages 25 and 40. Nine out of ten baby boomers say family is the most important thing in their lives. Yet this group also believes parents should pursue their own interests. For arts organizations, this translates to concurrent activities and/or child care. Often family interest can be aroused by offering a child-oriented activity. Museums, for example, often provide children's theme parties for birthdays and other occasions. But most museums do not actively encourage parents to explore while a party is going on.

The single woman needs to be viewed differently. Whether a boomer or of an older generation, she welcomes opportunities to meet new people. She'll look for surroundings that are safe, comfortable, and easily accessible when deciding whether to attend your events.

Think multigenerationally. With more Americans living longer, many families in the year 2000 will include four generations. Consider advertising and marketing campaigns to attract grandparents, parents, and children as a group. Spectator activities are excellent opportunities for the entire family to enjoy themselves together. Use ads and brochures that stress a mix of ages, colors, backgrounds, and tastes.

● **Work the corporate connection.** Several major corporations—among them SCM Corporation, Hitachi America Ltd., and Mobil—have increased their sponsorship of the arts. Their reason? An understanding that sophisticated purchasers base their buying decisions less on how products differ from each other than on how they view the companies that produce these products. Arts sponsorship polishes the image of a corporation. (A full discussion on cause-related marketing and corporate sponsorship can be found in Chapter 18.)

■ **Businesses marketing sporting events can adapt many of the recommendations for increasing fine and performing arts participation to their activities.** Here are some additional points to keep in mind, taken from a BBDO Media Research Report on women viewing network sports:

- **Highly-rated participatory sports do not necessarily do well as spectator sports.** Only two sports, horse racing (which is essentially spectator whether at the track or on TV) and bowling, were ranked in the top half of both bases in 1988.

- **While the total adult viewing audiences for network sports have been decreasing since 1983, women viewers have not declined as much as male viewers.** And since 1983, women 18+ (who make up 40 percent of the audience) have increased their spectator participation in seven sports events, the largest gainers being professional basketball, multi-sports events, and college football.

- **Only two sports, professional basketball and tennis, have increased their male 18+ viewing audiences.**

The conclusion for those mixing business with pleasure? If you plan to play in the leisure market, learn your demographics for a better performance!

CHAPTER FIFTEEN

Mining the Gold in Financial Products and Services

ACCUMULATING, SAVING, AND managing money will be major preoccupations for most of America in the years ahead. Living longer brings with it concerns about living well.

A Merrill Lynch survey of adults age 45 to 64 shows that 45 percent of the respondents say they are afraid they will outlive their money, and a whopping 69 percent see a risk of being overwhelmed by health care costs. Currently, most Americans say they save 1 to 20 percent of their income. And, while 23 percent of those surveyed report they are putting nothing towards retirement, 78 percent claim they'd save more if the government offered tax incentives.

Affluent adults of all ages and both sexes worry about the longevity of their assets. Forty-seven percent of women and 33 percent of men in households with annual incomes greater than $50,000 are "very" or "somewhat" concerned that they will outlive their retirement savings.* Providing for a comfortable retirement is the most commonly cited long-term financial goal in the planners' survey, and it is cited more often by higher-income households (35 percent) than by the general public (24 percent).

Retirement planning is becoming a concern of the relatively young. While older people worry more than the young about affordable medical care, a study by Money magazine

---

*A 1987 survey by the International Association for Financial Planning in Atlanta, Georgia.

shows that 41 percent of people under age 35 worry about whether they will have enough money for retirement.

The increasing preoccupation with financial planning offers great opportunities to those marketing and selling such products and services. The survey conducted by the International Association for Financial Planning also reveals that 80 percent of the general public—and 69 percent of households with annual incomes greater than $50,000—have never used financial planning services.

MARKETING TO FINANCIAL LIFESTYLES

Ken Dychtwald, in *Age Wave*, suggests that "when analyzing the financial styles of any particular generation, there are two basic issues to consider: whether they have money, and how do they feel about spending it." Not surprisingly, members of most cohorts form their core values with regard to how they relate to money during the influential years when they first start working.

Dychtwald says that today's 65+ consumers were deeply influenced in their youth by the terribly hard and financially frightening times of the Depression. Their point of view is "Save, save, save. Something terrible could happen, and you must be prepared for that rainy day."

In contrast, the next generation of elders, those who are today in their fifties and early sixties, were influenced by the great prosperity that followed World War II, as well as by the trying times of the Depression. Their point of view is a blend: "Save some, spend some."

Boomers were fully immersed as consumers in the free-spending, affluent decades following World War II, try as their parents did to inculcate in them a sense of financial practicality. Their point of view about money is thus somewhat different from that of their parents, and is totally at odds with that of their grandparents. Essentially, their attitude is this: "If you have no money in the bank, but have at least two credit cards that aren't over the limit, you're doing fine."

Keeping in mind Dychtwald's assertions about basic financial lifestyles, let's look at each of our four key demographic groups—baby boomers, the emerging Hispanic majority, aging Americans, and working women—to describe opportunities and marketing keys for "mining the gold" in financial products and services.

MARKETING FINANCIALLY TO BABY BOOMERS

Are baby boomers entering a new financial stage of life: shifting from consumption and the present to saving and the future? It depends on who you ask. Joseph McCarthy, president of the New York investment firm Lord Abbett, firmly believes that baby boomers are about to start the biggest investment boom ever. He points to the savings rate bounceback to 5.8 percent from its 3 percent 1987 low. Prudential-Bache predicts that the personal savings rate for this cohort should rise to about 10 percent.

McCarthy also suggests that unprecedented inheritances from the parents of boomers will accentuate the trend, swelling stock market averages as boomers inherit bonds and stock certificates from their income-oriented parents, and shift them to growth-oriented stocks. This makes sense when you review Ken Dychtwald's assessment of the boomer's financial style.

■ **Boomers may be receptive at younger ages than other groups to planning for retirement.** According to Jeff Ostroff, baby boomers—unlike today's prime-lifers, age 45 to 64—are more informed about the need to plan for retirement early. "They'll know, for example, that retirement could last 30 years or more, and that a long-term illness could wipe out all their savings. Tomorrow's prime-lifers will be unlikely to rest comfortably at night knowing they can depend on Social Security or Medicare in their later years. Tax increases, benefit cuts or freezes, and a growing imbalance between the ratio of workers to retirees may all fuel these doubts."

Ostroff believes the following will do well, as prime-lifers seek out specific services and products to help them and their families remain financially independent throughout the later years of life:

- Long-term care insurance

- Life insurance/long-term care insurance conversion policies

- Conservative savings/investment programs (blue-chip stocks, CDs, etc.)

Other areas aging baby boomers are likely to use:

- Pre-need trusts, pre-paid legal plans and paralegal services

- Investment newsletters and clubs

- Private pension plans, cash-flow analyses (of projected retirement assets), and payroll deduction plans

■ **Pre-market by addressing retirement concerns now.** In just a few short years, boomers will push the number of 50- to 64-year-olds from 33 million to a peak of 59 million in 2020, with the first of the boomers hitting traditional retirement age around 2011. "What we're seeing right now is the first stage of a rocket," says Charles Longino. "When the baby boomers start to buy, retirement markets are going to go into orbit."

Already, for example, there are long waiting lists for spaces in lifecare and other retirement communities. Boomers may be interested in securing their places earlier in life than previous generations.

But retirement is not the only boomer financial concern:

■ **Market to their concerns for providing for their children's college educations.** Because boomers married later and had children later, many—when they hit their fifties—will still be struggling with tuition payments. Robert Hewitt, president of the International Association of Financial Planners, believes that as the first broadly college-educated generation, boomers will save more than their parents did for their children's tuition. And they will do more of their savings and investing in mutual funds, rather than in individual stocks, bonds, or bank accounts.

Education is the biggest concern parents of children age three or younger have for their children's future, according to a survey by Gerber Products Company. Twenty-six percent of parents are concerned about the quality and cost of providing an education for their children.

And concerns about financing a college education rise with income, finds the American College Testing Program of Iowa City, Iowa, in a survey sponsored by *Money*. While 28 percent of all family decision-makers worry about college costs, this proportion rises to 45 percent among those with household incomes of $50,000 or more.

Savvy financial marketers are going to colleges and universities, suggesting partnerships that provide finder's fees to the school while benefiting alumni. The UCLA Alumni Association has become the first such organization to offer a program to assist parents in saving for their children's college education. The CollegeSure CD is especially appealing to mobile boomers, because it can be used at any college or university. The concept was developed by Paine Webber, Inc.

■ **Market to boomers as a "sandwiched" generation.** Robert Hewitt thinks the big shock to the boomer generation will not be the bills associated with their children, but those associated with their parents. Instead of the inheritances McCarthy envisages, Hewitt points to the long-term health care costs that could erase those inheritances.

■ **Market financial planning to reinforce the boomers' sense of "specialness."** In spite of—or because of—strong peer economic competition, many boomers live in a world where sophisticated financial planning is a mark of status. *Money, Inc.*, *Entrepreneur*—these magazines owe their success to a heavily boomer audience.

Not-for-profits and insurance companies have teamed up to market to this psychographic trigger. Colleges and universities are now inviting boomers to "make a relatively modest contribution today that matures into a major gift in the future" through a fund raising program that "establishes a trust fund with life insurance as the vehicle." The positioning in this new movement is important: a 45-year-old prospect can make a major gift of $50,000 for only $1,740 a year over a five year period, for a fully tax-deductible total pledge of $8,700. Boomers like financial vehicles which reinforce their sense of self.

Marketing Financially to Older Americans

Right now, although they represent only 25 percent of the total U.S. population, Americans over 50 have a combined annual personal income of over $800 billion, and control 70 percent of the total net worth of U.S. households—nearly $7 trillion of wealth. The over-50 group controls 50 percent of the discretionary income in the United States and 77 percent of the financial assets.

The "elderly" (age 65 to 74) receives 80 percent more income than average from estates, trusts, dividends, and rentals. The value of their assets is almost 21 percent greater than the average.

Households headed by people age 75 and over have income from estates, trusts, dividends, and rentals more than twice the average. The "aged" and the "very old" have assets with a value 5 percent above average.

Unlike the younger prime-lifer/baby boomer, says Jeff Ostroff, the more "senior" market's predominant concern will be the *management* of money. "For this reason, many older adults are likely to need the services of those who can help them oversee their assets, pay their bills, and protect their estates. Need for these services will be buoyed by the growth of the over-75 population, some of whom will be unable to handle these matters themselves but who will have the money to pay for them. Others, similarly unable, will have children willing to pay for the help."

Ostroff suggests these financial products and services are likely to be in demand by the senior population:

- Low-risk, income-producing stocks and bonds

- CDs, savings accounts, money market mutual funds, and government backed securities

- Medicare-supplemental and long-term care insurance policies

- Estate planning

- Income tax preparation

- Trust fund/portfolio management

Let's look at some marketing keys to use with older Americans:

■ **Market positively!** Especially when marketing financial planning to older Americans, we have a tendency to describe negative "what if" scenarios. Today's mature American is more likely to be interested in life income vehicles that enhance a comfortable retirement than a financial planning vehicle which saves inheritance taxes.

■ **Recognize they hold conservative attitudes towards money** and select financial institutions with guaranteed-safe investments, a high rate of return, and convenience as their priorities. They want to deal with people—not automatic teller machines. People age 50 and over tend to keep their money in several institutions, rather than consolidating their assets.

■ **Help them be more effective consumers** by offering financial seminars free of charge. Ostroff points out that a more educated older population "will thirst for information to help it function well in a rapidly changing marketplace. This will increase the desirability and marketability of those with specialized expertise in the areas of greatest interest to older consumers— particularly health care, financial services, and travel/leisure." Be sure to schedule your financial planning seminars in the daytime. Many older persons dislike driving at night because of vision problems.

■ **Help them guard their nest.** Often, older Americans have been widowed, divorced and remarried, or have a "significant other." Romance at later ages also brings with it concerns for protecting assets. Sensitive financial planning advice may be welcome by the entire family.

■ **Don't assume they won't purchase nest building vehicles.** Regardless of the level of income and assets, mature households' purchases of life insurance, endowments, and annuities are about the same as the national average, suggesting that mature consumers are still building estates.

■ **Work with not-for-profits to use financial planning for gift giving with tax advantages.** But the window of opportunity for major gifts from older Americans may be closing, cautions Robert F. Sharpe, a planned giving consultant to many charities. He says that "Changing demographics will have a tremendous effect on the amount and timing of giving in America for the rest of this century," and believes "We will increasingly be working with donors as they time their giving more carefully. The prime period for large gifts will be the period of time, in many cases very short, when family responsibilities have been met, homes paid for, and plans for retirement have been made."

■ **Seek out the "elder" newcomers to your community.** Many of the more affluent mature Americans "migrate" upon retirement to cities and towns that provide cultural, educational, and recreational opportunities. College towns, for example, are becoming choice retirement spots. Eugene, Oregon; Madison, Wisconsin; Austin, Texas; Ann Arbor, Michigan; Williamstown, Massachusetts; Ithaca, New York; Burlington, Vermont; Annapolis, Maryland; Charlottesville, Virginia; Hanover, New Hampshire; and Chapel Hill and Winston-Salem, North Carolina are showing significant growth in their mature populations. Work with realtors, chambers of commerce, and welcome wagons to find such individuals and help them get settled financially.

MARKETING FINANCIALLY TO WOMEN

Are you marketing your financial products and services heavily to women? You should. After all:

■ **Women outlive men.** *Women own 89 percent of the wealth of this country.* Women control the disposition of their own estates and, often, that of the spouse as well.

■ **Women are increasingly not marrying,** and are taking responsibility for their own retirements and estate planning.

■ **Women are becoming more affluent.** The numbers of women earning over $50,000 doubled from 1980 (6 percent) to 1986 (12 percent). As we continue into the twenty-first century, the gains will expand.

> While, as a group, women are "financially fairly savvy," many have not taken responsibility for handling their own financial resources. "Forty-one percent have never had a bank loan in their own names; 33 percent do not have their own checking accounts; 46 percent do not have savings and investment objectives; 44 percent have never personally made investments in stocks, bonds, mutual funds or real estate; 59 percent have no income-replacement options in the event they become disabled; a shocking 42 percent don't know their entitlements under their own and/or their spouse's Social Security and pensions; and *43 percent are without a financial plan to prepare for retirement.*" (According to a survey of its readership by *McCall's.*)

Women are a largely untapped market of opportunity for providers of financial products and services. Here are some marketing suggestions to consider:

■ **Market to women earlier.** Women are ready for financial advice at earlier and earlier ages. Begin to market to women in their mid-forties. Increasing numbers of more affluent women are remaining single, or become single at mid-life through divorce or widowhood. These women have greater earning potential in their own right, as well as continued traditional access to wealth from deceased family members. They are greatly concerned about providing for their own retirements and the eventual disposition of their assets. And many are the caregivers to parents and grandparents, handling financial responsibilities for multiple generations.

■ **Market specifically to affluent women.**

- Using *Standard and Poors, Who's Who in American Women*, etc., mark all women. Set appointments now.

- Get a list of all women donors who gave $5,000 or more to local not-for-profits. (They all print annual honor rolls of donors.)

- Follow up with all referrals of women even if, on the surface, they don't appear to be good prospects. Women have not been cultivated, by and large, and are often overlooked by the largely male financial planning community.

■ **Aim some prospecting strategies specifically at women.** You can't treat a woman just like a man. And many women are extremely sensitive to any perception of being patronized.

● **Provide women with resources.** Hold seminars and workshops on financial planning. Focus a segment on issues of concern for women. Show women in roles as financial advisors. Send a quarterly newsletter which focuses on retirement planning from the female perspective.

● **Educate your financial advisors to be sensitive.** Hold workshops for lawyers and trust officers with special segments on the concerns of women prospects. Women tend to be more conservative than men, often favoring less risky financial vehicles and looking for demonstrated fiscal accountability.

● **Write articles for local women's groups to include in their newsletters.** Include tax information and bequest information.

● **Prepare a talk on the subject of women and financial planning, and present it at women's service and professional organizations.**

● **Visit women.** Try to see all the women on your prospect list. (Take a few months and see *only* women. You'll be surprised at how much you've been concentrating on male prospects.)

■ **Understand and respect differing psychographics.**

● **The more traditional older woman may be motivated by a need for safety in her retirement planning.** She may not feel capable of dealing with her financial planning, and will trust your organization to "take care of her." She may also feel that, if your organization is one that was chosen by her late husband or father, she is continuing in a fashion they would approve. She'll expect your staff to be personal in its approach. For your communication vehicles: copy, graphics, and colors should be subdued.

● **Younger, career-oriented women are likely to be offended by marketing approaches that suggest they need to be taken care of.** They see themselves as decision-makers, setting a course of action that secures their own future. Appeal to their need to control the future. Suggest several different options. Your staff must project an air of equal partnership; communication vehicles should use crisper copy and bolder graphics, and might include examples of female role models addressing specific recommendations.

● **Women are your best prospects for charitable planned giving,** but prefer to honor others by their gift. The opportunity to pay tribute to a parent or other loved one is more likely to trigger a gift than a chance for personal recognition. *And be patient.* Recognize that many women are more concerned with their ability to replace gifts of wealth. Their first use of a life income vehicle will probably be modest.

Marketing Financially to Minority Populations

According to the experts, more than 90 percent of Hispanics agree that ''saving a portion of one's income is the best way to plan for the future'' and that ''it is essential for a man with a family to have life insurance.''

The Hispanic penchant for saving money and paying cash is good news for the insurance and banking industry. Yet minority populations are often ignored in marketing by financial institutions. As banks go after the larger depositor, many Hispanic-Americans feel their business is not appreciated. Although it is true that median incomes of minority households are often below that of white households, they have a variety of financial needs, from check cashing to money order purchases to tax preparation services.

■ **Carve out a niche that welcomes the modest dollar customers.** Enter Check-X-Change Corp., franchisor of America's largest and fastest-growing chain of check-cashing centers. It was recently named to the ''Franchisor 100'' list of *Venture* magazine. Check-X-Change caters to an estimated 15 to 20 percent of people who have no relationship with a bank, or whose schedules don't conform to regular banking hours. President Jeff Voss says, ''they're cookie jar people. These are people who choose not to have a banking relationship, or they are in areas where the service is not available,'' or they feel the bank doesn't want to spend much time on them because they're too small.

■ **Market using economies of scale.** Because Hispanic-Americans are younger than the national average, many of the key ''life events''—marriage and births, for example—lie ahead of them. They are likely prospects for insurance and conservative savings/investment vehicles. And while most are not affluent, marketing demographically can create the kind of economies of scale that make this market profitable.

■ **Make your organization welcoming.** Offer materials in both English and Spanish. Have financial planners who are conversant in both languages. Advertise in Hispanic publications.

■ **Market, psychographically, to Outer-Directedness.** Identify role models from the Hispanic community who can provide testimonials as to the value of financial planning. Let your prospects know they have been selected as community leaders and ask them to suggest other prospects.

■ **Respond to the sense of family.** Use direct response ads (remember, Hispanic Americans have the highest response rate to coupons) to invite parents to seek information on planning for children's educations. Or to discuss handling financial concerns with aging parents.

■ **Cultivate now for the years ahead** by increasing your organization's visibility with Hispanic constituencies. Offer complimentary financial planning sessions through the churches and fraternal and civic organizations. Become involved with the Hispanic community. Learn who the leaders and influential citizens are, and find out what needs you can meet.

SETTING THE STAGE FOR THE FUTURE

Financial products and services are an ideal example of the need to mesh high tech with high touch. Mark Gibson, of Retail Planning Associates in Columbus, Ohio, authored a study by the American Bankers Association, "Financial Retailing: Bank Branch Design and Merchandising," which states, "Most banks today look like museums. Tomorrow's banks will have to become stores in the truest sense of the word."

He foresees a time when customers will spend an afternoon in a living-room-like environment in a corner of their bank, watching their financial future on a giant TV screen and "trying on" different financial strategies like they would a coat.

Some financial institutions are already heading in this direction. Banking retailers consistently achieve 10 to 20 percent gains in sales and earnings each time they remodel or reconfigure their "stores," according to the ABA branch study. Apparently, customers enjoy the opportunity to "shop" at more futuristic branches. Banks undertaking new merchandising programs have experienced increased deposits, greater loan demand, and have gained new customers.

Bank One in Columbus, Ohio, and Dollar Dry Dock in New York, have created comfortable, boutique-like environments that allow customers to peruse services such as travel and stocks and bonds, and even to select, buy and pay for the house of their dreams at the same location.

Brightly lit, colorful environments generate feelings of speed and efficiency in the tellers' areas. Softer lighting and richer colors can be used in customer service and loan areas to encourage customers to relax and discuss their finances.

Features such as blue and pink neon signs, trendy posters, video displays, and larger-than-life murals and back-lit signs can all be used to communicate unique messages about the services your financial institution offers.

As you plan for the future, try positioning your organization to look inviting: more like a shopping gallery or community center than the marble and steel environment popular with most financial institutions today. All target groups should respond favorably to your attempts to make financial transactions "downright enjoyable."*

---

*William Tiberman, senior vice president of the Connecticut National Bank and vice chair of the ABA's Branch Administration Division.

PART IV

PLANNING YOUR MARKETING STRATEGY
FOR THE 1990S

Which businesses will flourish in the 1990s? Those that understand the nuances of marketing by demographics and psychographics. The reality is that there is often a curious gap between the realities of social change and social trends and the picture of society reflected in most marketing plans and in the advertising that expresses those plans. *Your organization can prosper in the coming decade by anticipating the trends and working with, rather than against, them.*

We've discussed the keys for targeting each of the key demographic groups. Now we'll explore how to use this information to formulate a cohesive marketing strategy that addresses the "triggers" of your best markets.

CHAPTER SIXTEEN

Where, Oh Where, Has the Loyal Customer Gone?

BEFORE YOU DESIGN a marketing program for your business, you need to understand and accept that your customers—and their buying habits—have changed dramatically.

■ **Customer loyalty is no longer the norm.** Today's consumers, according to the *Wall Street Journal*, are "a new breed of savvy consumers who put bargain prices, nutritional and environmental concerns, and other priorities ahead of old-fashioned brand loyalty."

Whether it's food or cosmetics, entertainment or clothing, items for the home or the road, more than half the 2,000 respondents to a *Wall Street Journal* survey said they're brand switchers.

People tend to be most loyal to brands that have distinctive flavors, such as cigarettes and toothpaste, or have a strong image associated with them, such as cigarettes, perfume or beer. Loyalty lags most for utilitarian products, such as trash bags or batteries.

Karen Olshan, a senior vice president at BBDO Worldwide ad agency, says "When there's a clutter of brands, consumers simplify the complexity by telling themselves, 'All brands are the same, so what difference does it make which I buy.' Too often, advertising imagery hasn't done a good job of forging a special emotional bond between a brand and the consumer."

Overall, according to Management Horizon's *Battle of the Brands*, those who care about brands tend to be disproportionately younger, affluent, and black. In softgoods categories, *designer brands* are most popular with urbanites, blacks, the young, and the affluent; *national brands* are most popular with older segments and middle to upper-middle class segments; *store brands* are, in general, more popular with the less affluent and the middle-aged range, but such profiles vary significantly according to the store brand.

In addition, according to *The Consumer's Perspective on Mass Market Shopping*, Americans across all income levels are evenly divided between those who pay full price on retail merchandise and those who wait for sales. While the inclination to wait for a sale is not gender specific, marital status does influence purchase behavior: 49 percent of single people will pay full price, while only 35 percent of marrieds will.

Middle-priced items are under pressure from both ends of the spectrum. They neither have the cachet of upscale goods nor the price pull of the discount brands.

● **Baby boomers are the least brand loyal of the emerging demographic populations.** They grew up with more brand choices than any generation, and have shown less allegiance so far. Peter Kim, of J. Walter Thompson, whose boomer demographic segmentation is described in Chapter 5, believes baby boomers will continue to be selective in their brand loyalty. "Earlier generations were brand loyal across categories," he says, "but boomers tend to be brand loyal in categories like running shoes and bottled water, but less so in others like toilet paper and appliances."

Boomers' early experiences may have conditioned them to disloyalty. For example, although better educated than the general United States population, boomers often do not support the colleges and universities they attended. Many believe that the college experience they received was not up to the expectations they had. The overcrowding and lack of individualized attention which was, in truth, a result of so many boomers crowding into a finite number of colleges and universities, has led to a lack of boomer "brand" loyalty to alma maters. *When a key life experience lets you down, it may form a pattern you continue when making purchasing decisions.*

● **Hispanic-Americans are, psychographically, the most brand loyal, but their actual buying habits reveal concerns.** Few organizations have seriously cultivated Hispanics; those that have find it difficult to change buying patterns. Campbell Soup Company, for example, fell short of anticipated sales when it acquired Casera Foods Inc., a Puerto Rico-based producer of Hispanic canned products. Hispanics remain extremely brand loyal to Goya Foods Inc., the New Jersey-based marketer and undisputed king of Hispanic foods, with a 65 to 90 percent market share in the food categories for which it competes.

Goya has a 50-year lead on Campbell. It has developed personal ties with the Hispanic market. "First and foremost, Goya has grown up with the Hispanic market," notes Bob Franklin, Goya's director of advertising and promotion. Adds Aldo Cunningham, Goya's director of sales: "We are service oriented; most American companies are consumption oriented."

Hispanic-Americans are often found at the lower end of the economic scale. Not surprisingly, the bottom end of the market is becoming less loyal. "They're buying whatever's cheaper."*

The Hispanic Car Market: Economic and Ethnic Realities, demonstrates the "tug" between loyalty and economics. While over three-quarters of Hispanic-Americans polled prefer to buy American cars—often because such automobiles are a status symbol in the countries from which they emigrated—the economics and demographics of U.S. Hispanics overpower these loyalties in car buying: they often buy imports.

---

*According to Laurel Cutler, vice chairman of the ad agency FCB/Leber Katz Partners.

An R.L. Polk & Company study credits three factors with bringing Hispanics to imports:

1. The heads of Hispanic households buying new cars are younger than their non-Hispanic equivalents (47.2 years versus 51.7).

2. Three-quarters of Hispanic households buying new cars have children at home, as opposed to just over half of non-Hispanic buyers.

3. The household income of Hispanic new car buyers is lower than that of non-Hispanic buyers (median $31,400 versus $35,900).

● **Older Americans are more brand loyal than the norm.** Nearly one-fourth of participants age 60 and over claimed brand loyalty for more than 10 of the 25 products in the *Journal* survey; only 9 percent of those age 18 to 29 have such strong allegiance.

However, not *all* older Americans are brand loyal. It is the truly "old," age 70 +, who continue patterns instilled in their youth.

● **Women are shifting their loyalties.** Traditionally, women have been the keepers of brand loyalty, passing it down from mother to daughter. Thirty-seven percent of wives are brand believers. These women are found in all age groups and in all employment statuses (although they are less likely to be service workers). However, those with high brand loyalty are more likely to view their work as a job, not a career. The DDB Needham research finds the brand believer to be a "typical, successful, satisfied, middle-class wife."

The changing role of women, from homemaker to partner or provider of the family's income, may contribute to a willingness to try new products and services. Working women spend less time choosing and using the household cleaning products and in food preparation than previously. Their identities are not as closely tied with their homes as are homemakers'.

● **Shifting psychographics** are also to blame. The key demographic groups have caused changes in the percentages of each VALS grouping:

	1983	1990	
● Needs-Driven	10%	11%	● heavily minority/ elderly
● Outer-Directed	68%	61%	● "mainstream" Americans
● Inner-Directed	19%	26%	● single women/ affluent boom- ers
● Integrateds	2%	4%	● still too small to tap

Psychographically, the growing numbers of Inner-Directeds and decreasing numbers of Outer-Directeds are hinting at even more brand disloyalty. Women, heavily represented among the Inner-Directed Experientials, have contributed to escalating concerns about nutrition and the environment. One consumer noted that after she heard about the artery-clogging hazards of tropical oils in many cookies, she dropped Pepperidge Farm and started buying brands free of such oils.

Battle of the Brands suggests these marketing responses to the loss of brand loyalty:

■ **Position your brand clearly.**

Trend	Brand Positioning
Time-scarce dual-income households	Brand names function as time savers.
Older and more educated consumers	Rely more on their own ability to evaluate products than they do on brand cues. Well-known alone isn't enough.
More secondary shoppers (like teens)	Will reach for well-known, familiar, advertised brands.
Fragmentation of consumer markets	More specifically targeted brands, particularly in the case of private store brands being in tune with core customers.
Growth in minority populations	Brand names function as a means of reducing risk, especially social risk, in particular among those who are less assimilated.
Income polarization	Upper end wants brands to function as time-savers rather than risk-reducers; the lower end will expect brands to function as reducers of financial risks.

■ Use Shopper Typologies to attract customers and consumers.

● *Utilitarian consumers* want things to last: Most are willing to pay more if they think a product will. For Utilitarians, brands facilitate shopping by providing convenience through price, durability, guarantees, familiarity, conformity and "comfort." They view designer brands as "wasteful and hedonistic." However, they can rationalize others buying designer brands because others have the income to do so, or as a treat. In order to attract and hold Utilitarians, it is important to promote brands' functional qualities.

● *Aesthetic consumers* want to avoid social risk; their choices must reflect their good taste and style. Brands facilitate shopping by providing options through quality, consistency with lifestyle, fashion/taste, excitement, self-expression, and "look." Designer brands are most desired, subject to budget limitations.

Research Alert concludes that "when retailers and manufacturers identify their core customers as either of these types, then all brand cues can be framed consistently toward maintaining and expanding the core, and preventing price comparisons."

Simply increasing communication is not the solution to creating customer loyalty. The need for more intensive communication is, unfortunately, a problem in and of itself.

CHAPTER SEVENTEEN

Taking the "Mass" Out of Your Marketing Strategy

TO DIFFERENTIATE YOURSELF from the market and build traffic and sales, you must use direct response vehicles (point of purchase displays and coupons; sales letters, flyers, and catalogs; and telephone sales) to reach prospects.

Unfortunately, you're not alone. Your competition is local, statewide, national, and—increasingly—global. Mailboxes are stuffed; television and radio stations glutted with appeals directed at your potential customer.

CUTTING THROUGH THE "COMMUNICATION" CLUTTER

Our overeager embracing of direct response vehicles may, in fact, be creating a backlash of resistance among today's more sophisticated prospects. Baby boomers, especially, who have grown up taking the marvels of computerization and communication for granted, are not fooled into believing "this message's just for you." Whether our vehicle is a "personalized" letter which inserts a prospect's name seven times in six paragraphs, or a phone call demonstrating the caller's familiarity with the prospect's consumption history, we increasingly hear that the results from direct response marketing are disappointing.

The heart of the problem lies in the boomers' view of themselves as special people. Having been told they are unique from early childhood, *boomers tend to see themselves as unique even when their level of involvement is modest or non-existent!* Boomers expect organizations seeking their patronage to cultivate them extensively. The dilemma is that direct marketing has been moving further and further away from true personalization.

In fact, marketers face similar problems in targeting each of the other key demographic groups: older Americans because they want to "get the full story" as suggested by *Modern Maturity*; Hispanic-Americans because they are Outer-Directed and looking for signs of group approval; and working women because they are aligning with products and services which fit their new image.

DIRECT MARKETING NEEDS TO INCORPORATE PSYCHOGRAPHICS

Forecaster John Naisbitt argued that high tech eventually forces people to demand high touch. ". . .whenever new technology is introduced into society, there must be a counterbalancing human response—that is, *high touch*—or the technology is rejected. The more high tech, the more high touch."

Naisbitt suggests that the nineties will require us to be more sensitive to marketing methodologies that provide the personal touch. Alex Kroll, CEO at Young & Rubicam, agrees. He feels that too many advertisers are ignoring individualism, a psychological trend that will gain importance in the next century. While most marketers may concur, the dilemma may be in learning how to manage this cost-effectively.

Using the services of an organization which can overlay psychographics to demographics can help (see Chapter 4).

While some marketers are putting renewed emphasis on image advertising, a small but growing number of companies are also trying to instill more fervent customer loyalty through such personalized direct marketing ploys as catalogs, magazines and membership clubs for brand users.

Others have decided to focus on their loyal buyers, rather than try to convert people who buy competing brands. Campbell Soup Company's vice president for marketing research, Tony Adams, believes "the best odds are with your core franchise. Our heavy users consume two to three cans of soup a week, and we'd like to increase that."

USING POINT-OF-PURCHASE, DIRECT MAIL,
AND TELEPHONE SOLICITATION

Once you decide who you will market to, demographically and psychographically, focus your direct response vehicles to get the best results. Each direct response vehicle—point of purchase displays, packaging, and coupons; direct mail letters, flyers, and catalogs; and telemarketing—can be made stronger by your understanding of what triggers the key consumer groups.

■ **People enjoy shopping.** Next to home and office, Americans spend the most time in shopping malls. According to John Naisbitt, "Computer buying will never replace the serendipity and high touch of shopping for what we want to be surprised about." Impulse buying is one of the joys of on-site shopping.

■ **Location, location, location—still the key to retail success.** Francesca Turchiano, writing in *American Demographics*, suggests that "the great shopping mall shakeout of the 1990s is just beginning." As many as 20 percent of the regional shopping centers now operating in the United States will close by 2000, and the decline will continue into the twenty-first century.

A key demographic reason for the predicted decline: an aging population. In addition to value, security, quality, comfort and convenience, socialization and recognition are the key intangibles in selling to mature consumers. With the exception of security, these intangible qualities sought by older adults are not easily found in a shopping center environment.*

Rather, Turchiano predicts that unenclosed shopping centers anchored by one-niche megastores such as Toys R Us and off-price centers will succeed, as well as smaller shopping areas which target specific population groups.

Convenience, not price, is the motivating factor for people age 50 and over when they decide where to shop and what to buy, according to a study by MERETRENDS, the consulting service of Retail Planning Associates and Ernst & Whinney of

---

*According to the Donnelley Marketing's 1989 study of the mature market.

Columbus, Ohio. Seventy-one percent say they would pay more for merchandise if it were sold closer to their homes.

■ **Point-of-purchase displays and packaging should focus on providing information, while stressing convenience and health.** *Research Alert* reports that Americans over age 65 not only want more nutrition and health information on food and pharmaceutical packages, they also prefer words rather than color coding for clues to such things as decaffeinated or regular coffee. The general aging of the American population suggests that displays and packaging should both use larger type. Because boomers and single working women have concerns about the environment, a sensitivity to packaging will be appreciated.

■ **Coupon use follows demographics.** Consumers in the United States were bombarded with almost 210 billion coupons in 1986 alone. According to a report in *American Demographics*, "money-back coupons are most popular among people who earn more than $60,000 per year, and least popular with those earning less than $15,000. More than half of the consumers between the ages of 35 and 44 use coupons, while fewer than one-third of those under age 25 and over age 65 clip them."

Early studies suggested that blacks and Hispanics were more likely to be brand-loyal, and therefore less likely to use coupons than whites. But a study done in 1988 by Donnelley Marketing reveals that approximately 88 percent of Hispanic households redeem coupons, compared to 77 percent for the U.S. average. Findings from a report published by the Lempert Company of Belleville, New Jersey, suggests that coupon use is increasing faster among Hispanics than among other segments of the U.S. population. Donnelley Marketing finds that 47 percent of Hispanic coupon users redeem five or more coupons a week. More than two-thirds of Hispanics redeem three or more coupons per week compared to 59 percent for the country as a whole. A reader survey by *Vista*, the Sunday newspaper supplement for Hispanics, found that 48 percent of Hispanics "almost always" use coupons, while 42 percent "sometimes" use them.

■ **Mail and phone sales—as opposed to point of purchase sales —will continue to grow.** In 1983 there were some 57.4 million consumers who shopped by mail or phone, according to Simmons Market Research Bureau. By 1989, that number had grown to 91.7 million. While the population grew by 12.5 percent in that six year period, the number of American adults who shopped by mail or phone increased by 59.7 percent. Some of the fastest growing mail order categories are apparel, videocassettes, business supplies, and health (drugs/vitamins/ fitness) products, as well as consumer electronics and computer software.

● **Busy Americans are buying more by catalog and from ads.** *More than 70 percent of people age 50 and over order at least one item by mail or telephone each year,* according to a study by Goldring & Company of Chicago. Clothing, books, seeds and plants, records and tapes, hobby and craft items, housewares, vitamins, and film developing are the most popular mail-order items for this group.

● **Fifty-five percent of college students** make purchases by mail or phone. They order records, tapes or compact disks (48 percent), followed by books (45 percent), casual clothing (27 percent), video tapes (22 percent), sporting goods (17 percent), and audio equipment or photo supplies (15 percent).

● **Baby boomers,** it's being suggested, will buy more by mail and phone as they move more heavily into "cocooning." A 1988 *Newsweek* poll showed that Americans generally were "almost three times more likely than they were in June 1986 to say that 'staying home with family' is their favorite way of spending an evening." The group most likely to want to stay at home, according to *Newsweek*, was age 30 to 49. Federal Express, UPS Three Day Delivery, phone ordering, and the FAX machine all work to encourage boomers to order from the couch.

However, people age 30 to 59, those with high incomes, and professionals are most likely to throw out direct mail without opening it! An idea to try: put an outstanding testimonial on the outer flap of your envelope. There is no way to avoid seeing it.

A M E R I C A N

VOICES

GET THE MESSAGE People aged 30 to 59, those with high incomes, and professionals are most likely to throw out direct mail without opening it.

(percent of all adults who say they usually throw out direct mail without opening it, by age, income, and occupation)

Total. 38%

AGE

18 to 29 . . . . .33%

30 to 44. .40

45 to 59 41

60 and older 37

INCOME

Less than $15,000. . . . . .34%

$15,000-$24,999 33

$25,000-$34,999. 35

$35,000 and over 43

OCCUPATION

Professionals/executives. 48%

White-collar employees 38

Blue-collar employees 31

Source: The Roper Organization. 1989

Reprinted with permission ©American Demographics, December 1989.

■ **Direct mail won't work if your techniques are behind the times.** Herschell Gordon Lewis warns that ''we're mired deep in the Age of Skepticism, and the reader looks down on entertainers. . . .In the 1990s we walk the tightwire. We aren't professorial and we aren't buffoons. We grab and hold attention with 1990s techniques such as handwriting; we write a readable letter, neither fawning nor supercilious, neither doltish nor standoffish."

● **Older Americans are the most direct mail responsive of our demographic segmentations.** But not *all* older Americans respond the same. Jerry Huntsinger, often referred to as the "Dean of Direct Mail," differentiates among older Americans, based on their responsiveness to solicitations by mail:

> • The **"Old"**, **age 70+** , are strongly direct mail responsive. Heavily female, they have faith in American business. For them, direct mail is an invitation to adventure.
>
> • The **current old, age 65+** , are *not* direct mail responsive. They have higher educations and higher cynicism, having lived through two decades of racial riots, Vietnam, and televangelism. This reminds us that not just boomers were affected by the turbulent sixties and seventies.
>
> • The **new old, age 55+** , are the most direct mail responsive because of having been conditioned by the massive direct-response industry.

■ **Consider including a "handwritten note" with your appeal.** *Sixty-eight percent of Americans prefer this personalization.* Women respond more positively than men (72 percent versus 64 percent). People's attitudes toward handwritten materials suggest that direct marketers should incorporate the look in their pieces. "Handwritten notes make direct-mail pieces look less mass produced and more like a human being had a hand in their creation," says David Watson, fund raising director for the Southern Poverty Law Center in Montgomery, Alabama. Watson uses handwritten notes inside and out on his direct-mail pieces. Sometimes his group reproduces entire letters from constituents in its mailings because of the power of a handwritten note.

■ **Videologs could be the tool of the future.** The continued growth in catalog shopping and shopping via video will alter the appearance of packages shown in these media. Richard Gerstman, speaking on "Packaging in the 1990s" at the 1988 EastPack conference, notes, "Instead of being designed to compete on crowded shelf sections, packages would have to sell products via the two-dimensional page of the catalog, and the not-quite two- or three-dimensional representation on the video screen. In both cases, packages would be seen in more glamorous settings and without hundreds of competitors, as in most retail environments. Different design and marketing objectives would determine their appearance."

Scandinavian Ski Shop is already offering a 30 minute videolog which accompanies a printed catalog. After briefly introducing the company, the video shows eighty different outfits in action ski shots and tight-frame close-ups for detail. Shot on location at ski resorts, the ski fashions are keyed to background music and breathtaking scenery.

Jo-Von Tucker, a respected direct marketer, reviewed the Scandinavian Ski Shop videolog in *Direct Marketing* magazine:

> It is a marketing communication that provides the customer with fun, excitement, entertainment, information, edited product selection and the convenience of ordering by telephone, toll-free...(the videolog) has put the *fun* back into catalog shopping. You feel like you are there, experiencing the thrill of downhill, the tranquility of cross country, and even the super high of heliskiing and snowboarding. And, more important from a marketing perspective, you really want to look exactly like the models do as they flash by...What is of vital interest is that the consumer is totally caught up in the experience. By effectively creating the feeling of 'being there,' the videolog attains credibility for the company, while presenting the merchandise under ideal and desirable circumstances. It motivates the customer to make a purchase!

■ **Personalized telemarketing works better than direct mail or phone solicitation alone.** Borrow a technique from the not-for-profit world: combine direct mail and telephone solicitation to make sales soar! Often referred to as telecommunications programs, rather than telemarketing, such approaches use a pre-approach letter to let the prospect know he or she will be receiving a phone call in the near future. The letters are often long—three pages—and provide detailed information on what you want your prospect to do (buy a product, agree to see a salesperson, receive more literature, take a trial subscription, etc.). The phone call assumes that the solicitation has been made in the letter and the caller is a facilitator, trained to answer questions and move the prospect towards a decision. This methodology can be especially effective when used to reconnect lapsed consumers—subscribers to magazines, merchandise of the month clubs, and sports or performance season ticket holders—and works equally well with educating new consumers—financial planning materials, expensive durable goods purchases, and purchases demanding a complex explanation or lengthy decision-making.

MARKET GLOBALLY, NOT LOCALLY

Walt Disney was right in suggesting "it's a small, small world." *Business Tokyo*, the English-language magazine that covers the commercial front in Japan, says the 10 fastest-growing foreign firms in Nippon are: 1) Amway, 2) Bayer, 3) DuPont, 4) Dow Corning, 5) Dow Chemical, 6) Boehringer Ingelheim, 7) Upjohn, 8) Imperial Chemical, 9) General Electric, and 10) Bristol-Myers.

Clearly, the United States still makes many things the world wants. Whether it's computers, airplanes, blue jeans, American films or American music—the market for many American-made products extends far beyond our borders. And Jerome W. Pickholz, chairman of Ogilvy & Mather Direct, suggests that needs and wants around the world are becoming increasingly similar.

If yours is a product or service which can attract similar demographic or psychographic groups around the world, consider marketing globally. Assuming you can answer positively the questions, "Do we want consumers worldwide to view our products the same way? Should they? Is a single global positioning desirable?" Pickholz argues persuasively that you will find the world made of market segments which appear in different countries or regions at the same time:

Indeed, a perfect example that I've found are participants of worldwide conferences I attend. They come from many different countries: Japan, Korea, Brazil, Western Europe and so on. But we are a market segment. We are a culturally convergent group. I'll tell you how I would describe us. We are likely to be age 30 to 55, man or woman:

- Wear a Christian Dior shirt or blouse, Bally or Gucci shoes.

- Carry a Hartman suitcase containing a bottle of duty-free Glenlivet Scotch whiskey.

- Use Paco Raban cologne or wear a Hermes scarf.

- Own a Sony radio, TV and VCR.

- Write with a Gold Cross pen.

- Read *The Economist*.

- Pay with an AmEx card (presumably Gold) and travellers checks.

- Document a trip with a Canon camera.

- Consult a Rolex watch.

- Drive a Mercedes, BMW or other high-performance car.

- Travel first-class, stay at the best hotels, and be a member of various airline travellers clubs.

I may have some brand names wrong, but how far off am I? And it makes no difference what country they come from. *I've identified a group by lifestyle, not by country of origin.* (Italics added for emphasis.)

As we move through the 1990s, the rapid growth of high tech and globalization increases the trend toward increased market segmentation. Savvy marketers will work their niches and segments demographically and psychographically to enhance success.

CHAPTER EIGHTEEN

"Psyching Out" Your Customer

MANY PRODUCTS AND SERVICES demand high touch. Although we may be willing to shop electronically for staple items, or those for which we have a very clear sense and experience, we want to connect with other people when we purchase items and services which either cost a lot or reinforce our sense of identity.

■ **Especially if your product or your service is a discretionary purchase with a high price tag attached to the decision to buy, what type of marketing strategy is most useful?** Your first need is to find who, *demographically*, is most likely to buy your products and/or services. You can then refine your prospect pool by matching the *psychographics* of those prospects with your current and past customers/consumers.

And you'll want to do some testing; just because your business has never drawn well from one or more of our four key groupings doesn't mean that affluent boomers, Hispanic-Americans, older Americans, and/or working women aren't good prospects. It may mean that your approach has not turned lookers into buyers.

Assuming one or all of these demographic cohorts turns up in your prospect pool, you'll find the marketing keys for each demographic group provided in Chapters 5–8 can help you decide on your image campaign strategy, media placement, point of purchase atmosphere, and the types of sales brochures you will offer. These chapters will also help in guiding the sales dialogue.

- **And there's good news—affluent Americans are among the most loyal of constituencies.** Higher income people tend to be more loyal customers and consumers. According to a *Wall Street Journal* survey, and other research studies, "Marketers speculate that more affluent people tend to lead more pressured lives and don't have time to research the products they buy for the highest quality and the most reasonable price. An established brand name is insurance that at least the product will be of acceptable quality, if not always the best value for the money. It's sort of loyalty by default."

  Even if your product is not a recognized brand, you can benefit from the more affluent consumer's loyalty. But you must get the customer's attention before you worry about followup and repeat sales.

- **Let's assume you've identified the right group of prospects and have now gotten them in the door.** Unfortunately, many of our sales staff working the floor don't understand the "triggers" that can move the prospect along. Psychographic screening can suggest *how* to structure the cultivation and solicitation process for these persons most effectively.

  (**Note:** Usually the not-for-profit world takes from the business world. This chapter works in reverse. It uses successful major gift fund raising techniques as a basis for its assumptions.)

- **The first step: working together.** The relationship between the salesperson and the prospect cannot be adversarial. Your salesperson must be a facilitator, making the prospect feel good about relinquishing power (money) for a benefit (purchase). This "voluntary exchange of benefits," cited by Philip Kotler in *Marketing for Nonprofit Organizations,* is marketing. No matter how excellent your product or service, the sale will not be made if the needs and goals of your prospect (both tangible and intangible) are not met.

By using psychographics, the salesperson can pinpoint the values, attitudes, and lifestyle particulars that will facilitate quicker decision-making on the part of the prospect.

LIMITATIONS OF FORMAL PSYCHOGRAPHIC SCREENING

The most sophisticated of the psychographic profiling measures is the VALS double hierarchy described fully in Chapter 3. That chapter also suggests alternative systems. These systems work extremely well in helping you learn who your current customers and consumers are, using survey methods to request information which can be tabulated. They are also helpful in directing your media advertising and the "look and feel" of your store. But they do not provide you with a "reality check" when the customer or consumer walks through the door.

How do you know if Ms. or Mr. Brown will prefer an "Inner-Directed" versus "Outer-Directed" sales presentation? The answer is: you don't. Recognizing that reality, I developed a "quick and dirty" psychographics labelling process which I find works well in face-to-face situations.

NICHOL'S PERSONALITY THEORY: AN ALTERNATIVE

THE THREE KEY PERSONALITY TYPES

Visualize a bell-shaped curve. The majority of your prospects will fall in the center of the curve. These people are "members of the herd." Those who can be placed to the extreme left are "innovators." To the extreme right, "laggards." Once classified as "innovators," "members of the herd," or "laggards," prospects can be matched up with an appropriate approach, and, when there is a choice among products or services your organization offers, guided towards those that fit better with their self-image. Doing so will help you find the "trigger" that leads to more significant purchases *and* a quicker close.

Note: Innovators, members of the herd, and laggards are both males and females. For brevity's sake, I will use the pronouns "he" and "him."

■ **Innovators** look to be in the forefront. They want the opportunity to set new directions, to encourage others, to play a leadership role. They are often idealistic and impulsive. They expect to be approached by representatives of stature. Innovators are good prospects for "new and improved" products. They are often willing to buy from a prospectus or before the product is in stock because they like feeling they are getting in on the ground floor. Draft documents and xeroxed memos, sketches rather than formal graphics, and unmounted photographs are of more interest than a polished brochure.

Innovators need to be involved in the planning process and often enjoy playing an active role in choosing purchases. An articulate spokesperson can quickly ignite their enthusiasm but, often, innovators have short attention spans. They show little loyalty and will move on to other organizations if their products and services appear "newer and better." Your salesperson will feel confident s/he's made the sale, but if s/he can't move to a quick close, you often lose the innovator. You can't "get back" to an innovator: you must anticipate requests, providing immediate followup and a push for quick decision-making.

Innovators go on instinct. They "like" something or don't. Because they tend to be the busiest of individuals, they don't want to be kept waiting. Also, they like dealing with people in authority from the beginning, not being passed from salesperson to sales manager.

"Making a deal" matters to the innovator, more as a demonstration of how to work the system to best advantage than as a need. Often an innovator will offer complicated scenarios just because the mechanics appeal to him.

Innovators like recognition, and won't be shy in suggesting what they would like. They seek publicity and will be willing, even eager to serve in your advertisements as spokespersons, or giving testimonials.

■ **Members of the herd,** unlike bold innovators, need to be reassured that others have already made the decision to purchase your product or service. They get reassurance from knowing you've been endorsed by others. It's *sequential selling.*

Members of the herd want to be part of the "in" crowd; peer acceptance is very important. They will often ask "who's bought already." Formal advertisements with testimonials are important to provide a stamp of approval. If a respected peer or an admired colleague endorses your products and services, members of the herd will quickly follow. Herd prospects respond best when you can indicate that "Joe sent me."

While innovators tend to laugh at traditional recognition vehicles, members of the herd take visible signs of their status very seriously. Membership cards, key rings, a "VIP" phone number for service—these are important to members of the herd.

If you visit prospective clients, you'll find members of the herd provide excellent visual "clues": if a prospect's office or home walls are covered with citations, prominently displayed, you are probably dealing with a member of the herd.

■ **Laggards** take their time in deciding whether or not to buy from you. They look for visible signs of success—positive articles in the press, letters of endorsement—before making a commitment. Laggards save each issue of *Consumer Reports* and refer to it before setting forth to purchase.

Laggards look for consistency. They come to your business knowing exactly what they want, and get annoyed if your salesperson suggests alternatives or options. Whereas innovators like feeling that buyer and seller are partners "creating the right package," laggards want the salesperson to agree with the laggard's choice and help to implement that without change.

A laggard can be frustrating to the salesperson; they often seem to take forever to make up their minds to buy. But, once they do decide, they are the most loyal of customers. They take pride in having used your products and services time and time again.

Laggards expect you to recognize that they're steady, dependable customers. Greeting them by name is important. However, laggards are not usually concerned with tangible forms of recognition. They don't seek publicity, but can be persuaded to give testimonials if approached with sensitivity.

■ **Innovators, members of the herd, and laggards all provide clues to their psychographic profiles.** Clues to a prospect's personality can be found in:

- History of behavior (yours and competitor's)

- Lifestyle preferences in other areas (cars, travel, dress, entertainment)

- Choice of profession

- Stage of life (children at home, retiree)

People can shift psychographically depending on whether they are a customer or consumer. A prospect could be an innovator in purchases for himself but a laggard when buying for a child.

It's always tempting to try to find a predominating psychographic profile for a demographic cohort. Resist it. Once you start to deal with people in face to face situations with assumptions in hand, you stop listening to them and learning what their needs are. When you're dealing with products or services which people can choose to do without, or for which the choices they make are closely aligned to the image that product or service projects, let your prospects be your guide!

CHAPTER NINETEEN

New Kid on the Block: Cause-Related Marketing

YOU WANT—AND NEED—to reach the lucrative constituencies of baby boomers, Hispanics, aging Americans, and working women. But often, the experiences of these target consumers have left them doubting the companies courting them. In a society which no longer trusts business or government, not-for-profits—religious charities, educational institutions, medical foundations, environmental organizations, the fine and performing arts, youth and social service agencies, and human benefit programs—still have credibility. This has led to a surge of partnerships between business and not-for-profits.

MAKING CORPORATE SUPPORT A WIN-WIN PARTNERSHIP

Whether you accept it as philanthropy or label it as marketing, profit-motivated giving (more frequently called cause-related marketing, a term copyrighted by the Travel-Related Services unit of the American Express Company) is the area of growth for many corporations, and increasingly, for small businesses as well.

There are more than one million not-for-profit organizations in the United States. Many are in your community. All are eager for funding partners. Don't assume only the large corporation can effectively find a not-for-profit partner. Interest from all companies—big and little, established and new—will be welcomed.

Originally, corporate philanthropy was a voluntary response to social issues and problems. Over the centuries, it evolved into mandated corporate involvement. Corporate philanthropy now appears to be evolving into a phase in which social responsibility is viewed as an investment by both large and small businesses.

"America's business leaders say they remain committed to the concept of corporate philanthropy, but they are more and more likely to ask how a gift will contribute to their companies' goals before reaching for their checkbooks," reports *The Chronicle of Philanthropy*. *The NonProfit Times* agrees, noting that "Market yourself" is becoming a common warcry, as not-for-profits seek to demonstrate what they can do for a corporation. While some corporate leaders like Peter Goldberg, former vice president, public responsibility, at the Primerica Corporation, are concerned that the trend "injects an element of crassness into philanthropy that is troubling," far more common is the attitude of Timothy McClimon, vice president for arts programs at the AT&T Foundation. He believes that the convergence of marketing and philanthropy can be healthy if it is "done with everybody's eyes open."

USING CAUSE-RELATED MARKETING EFFECTIVELY

Because cause-related marketing is a versatile tool, it can be used to realize a broad range of organizational and marketing objectives. For example:

- gaining national visibility

- enhancing corporate image

- thwarting negative publicity

- pacifying customer groups

- increasing brand awareness

- increasing brand recognition

- enhancing brand image

- broadening customer base

- reaching new market segments and geographic markets

According to a survey by Independent Sector, both companies and not-for-profits are pleased with their experiences, and plan to continue their activities. Both sides expect to see more for-profit support of special events such as concerts, walkathons, and sports tournaments. Alcohol, tobacco, and pharmaceutical companies, for example, that may feel direct-purchase incentives (such as coupon redemptions) are inappropriate for their products, find sponsorships ideal.

With receptive business leaders encouraging not-for-profits to bring ideas to them, the profit-motivated-giving pocket of corporate philanthropy and marketing is clearly going to grow. *The Philanthropy Report*, a Seattle-based newsletter, estimated that marketing-based corporate arts support equaled nearly $500 million in 1988, for the first time exceeding the amount expected to be donated through philanthropy, which it put at $470 million.

■ **A key to using cause-related marketing properly is to "know your needs."** You need to find not-for-profits whose constituencies mirror key demographic segments—whether boomers, Hispanics, older Americans, or working women—or have psychographic appeal to those with the lifestyles, values and attitudes your company is seeking. Ask your potential partners to provide clear examples of how their organizations are perceived positively by the target group(s) and evaluate carefully what the organization wants and can do. Warner Canto, vice president of special projects for American Express, rightfully decries the many cause-related marketing programs that have been "poorly conceived," featuring "inappropriate causes" and "ill-defined objectives." He urges businesses to apply the same marketing disciplines to cause-related marketing programs as they do to other marketing efforts, and calls for not-for-profits to become better marketers.

■ **Cause-related marketing works for *all* demographic targets.**

● *Cause-related marketing lends itself to boomer "triggers" like nostalgia and music.* Cause-related marketing which mirrors how boomers see themselves will, most likely, receive enthusiastic welcome.

Cause-related marketing combines traditional and non-traditional values well:

> Bob Geldof, the Irish rock musician whose Band Aid raised $110 million for the relief of African famine, demonstrated how responsive boomers will be when touched properly. Combining the boomer values of globalism and family with their love of music, and the assurance that "every cent you give goes to the cause" proved the key in motivating a constituency most had ignored. Michael Norton, who heads London's Directory of Social Change, suggests that Band Aid "didn't need to raise money. The news media, especially TV, raised it for them. Band Aid just needed to provide a channel for the money to flow in."

Cause-related marketing appeals to boomers' fondness for the 1950s and 1960s:

> Seeking to update its image, Wisk detergent joined forces with local festivals, fairs and special events to provide a 24-minute fireworks display which concluded with a special "ring around the sky" symbolizing the famous Wisk "Ring around the Collar" ad theme. The fireworks were choreographed to the music of 30 years of rock and roll.

A more subtle approach to baby boomers might focus on their life stages. Masco, a major Michigan corporation with subsidiaries in home furnishings, noted in its 1989 annual report that it was "Targeting the Future...," suggesting it was sure to do well because of baby boomers; because they were better educated, at the peak of their earnings capacity, and because of the boomers' "cocooning" phenomenon. If, like Masco, you are selling home-related products or services, isn't there logic in sponsoring quality public television broadcasting—at-home upscale entertainment? Or addressing boomers' fitness needs by funding medical research on back pain and furniture at a school of medicine? Or working with boomer concerns by providing furniture for a daycare or elder care center?

● *Cause-related programs send a message of "inclusion" to Hispanics and other audiences who are wary.*

Art and music may be the best bridge for reaching the Hispanic American market. McDonald's sponsored a Hispanic Heritage Art contest in the mid-1980s. Brochures promoting the contest were distributed to bilingual education teachers in Hispanic communities throughout the United States. The Capital Children's Museum in Washington, D.C., displayed the prize-winning entries, and grand-prize winners presented their drawings to the president of the United States during Hispanic Heritage Week. More recently, Coors sponsored a two-year tour of Hispanic art throughout the country. Pepsi-Cola and Coca-Cola both have sponsored Hispanic music awards, and Pepsi features Miami Sound Machine, a well-known Hispanic group, in its commercials.

Among the recent projects sponsored by the AT&T Foundation is a traveling exhibit of Hispanic art, the first major exhibit of Hispanic work to go into mainstream museums. The support was given for "good reasons," but there is "no denying the Hispanic population is important in the marketplace," says Timothy McClimon, who adds that AT&T has professionals dedicated solely to marketing to Hispanics.

Philip Morris Companies Inc. is sponsoring "The Latin

American Spirit: Art and Artists in the United States, 1920-1970.'' The tour moves from the Bronx, New York to El Paso, Texas to San Diego, California to San Juan, Puerto Rico to Vero Beach, Florida—all major concentrations of Hispanic Americans. Why is Philip Morris doing this? Possibly because Hispanic Americans are the youngest of target groups, prime potential consumers of tobacco products.

Marrying art and culture with customer outreach is fairly common in cause-related marketing. More unique is another attempt to reach the Hispanic American community by Frito-Lay. *American Demographics* reports that Frito-Lay "is building brand awareness—literally—in Hispanic neighborhoods. It is using hammers and nails instead of coupons and advertisements. Its goal is to build playgrounds, to promote good will, and last but not least, to sell more snacks.''

> In 1971, Frito-Lay dropped its symbol, the Frito Bandito, after hearing from Hispanic groups who found the character demeaning. In 1987, seeking a project to rebuild its relationship with the Hispanic-American community, Frito-Lay launched the "Parque de la Amistad" playground program by building its first "Friendship Park" in Hidalgo Park, a predominantly Hispanic neighborhood in Houston.
>
> "We wanted to increase overall Frito-Lay awareness among Hispanics. Our market research shows that Hispanics tend to be very brand-loyal," says Beverly Holmes, spokeswoman for Frito-Lay in Plano, Texas. Recognizing that Hispanics are family-oriented, Frito-Lay decided to do something for Hispanic children. As Holmes notes, "a coupon lasts for a week or two. A playground lasts for generations.''

Other companies have responded to Hispanic Americans' love of soccer. Most American communities with large Hispanic populations have local soccer leagues for both youth and adults. The Ford Motor Company sponsors amateur soccer in the United States, enlisting the world-famous soccer player Pele, of Brazil, as a celebrity spokesperson. In 1994, when the U.S. hosts soccer's World Cup, Ford will reap a publicity bonanza among Hispanics.

And consider Miami Toyota dealer Richard Goldberg, who has poured thousands of dollars into Latin community events, including beauty pageants, the annual Calle Ocho festival in Little Havana, as well as youth baseball and soccer teams. "Give me a Cuban holiday and we'll sponsor it," jokes Goldberg. Expressway Toyota's sales have climbed 400 percent in six years as a result of savvy marketing to Miami's Hispanic community.

● *Older Americans are not being ignored* by companies seeking cause-related ventures. Masters and senior tournaments of golf and tennis are on the upswing. Opportunities await the company who partners with a not-for-profit who can reach subsegments within the mature market.

McDonald's is possibly the most demographically-aware of American corporations. Their commercials now segment out older Americans both as consumers and as employees. A marketing representative from McDonald's was recently asked if any plans existed for a Ronald McDonald House for the spouses and families of the elderly dealing with catastrophic illness. While no specifics have been agreed upon, she indicated that McDonald's was looking for projects along that line.

● *Women's more personal focus has identified different cause-related marketing directions.* Johnson & Johnson wanted to create a group promotion event that would have maximum consumer "pull" with women—the key consumers for Johnson & Johnson products. Keying in on boomer women, a campaign focusing on the issue of domestic violence was created. Called "Shelter Aid," the program combined an outright donation from Johnson & Johnson to establish and operate a toll-free domestic-violence hotline, with consumer involvement via coupon redemption and point-of-purchase donation canisters. An extensive public relations program featured actress Lindsay Wagner.

- **Cause-related marketing can be psychographically driven.** *Sometimes, corporations and businesses are better served by defining potential consumers in terms of shared similar attitudes.* Rather than demographics, psychographics are used as the key to choosing a not-for-profit partner. Your business must look for a not-for-profit organization which can suggest a project to which groups of dissimilar Americans might react in a like fashion.

  MasterCard, for example, encouraged its cardholders to be involved in the allocation of funds among several charities using a balloting process. "Choose to Make a Difference" benefits the Alzheimer's Association, American Cancer Society, American Heart Association, American Red Cross, Just Say No Foundation, and the National Committee for Prevention of Child Abuse. MasterCard hoped to enhance its image (and increase card usage) with those individuals most likely to respond positively to being involved in directing MasterCard's charitable giving. Concerns about stewardship are typical of Outer-Directed Achievers and Inner-Directed Societally Conscious—the highest income VALS groupings and key users of credit cards.

  Similarly, Spiegel, Inc. has used cause-related marketing to increase catalog sales. Spiegel donates 33 cents from each order it receives from a "Holiday Thrills" gift collection catalog marketed during Christmas to selected charities.

- **Environmental concerns may be the "hot" cause-related marketing issue for the 1990s.** We're seeing the start of "the Green Revolution." The 1990s may well be the Aware Decade, when "every purchase made by family and by business will be influenced not just by price, convenience and profit, but by the product's effect on life on earth," asserts writer Joel Makower.

  Environmental protection is emerging as a "consensus issue." "Concern about ecological issues is no longer associated primarily with younger, better-educated people who were in the vanguard of the environmental movement two decades ago," says the *Gallup Report.* "Today, environmentalists comprise a broad-based coalition from diverse social and economic backgrounds."

Already, partnerships are being formed. Television shows such as "thirtysomething" are speaking out on environmental issues, due in part to meetings between the show's writers and the Environmental Media Association. And, interviewed on the eve of his 1990 World Tour, Paul McCartney emerged as an environmental spokesman and guardian of the ecology: "Linda and I decided we could go out, have fun entertaining the fans and make a bit of money," he says. "Or we could do all that and something worthwhile at the same time. Environmental concerns were a logical choice for us."

■ **While most cause-related marketing is focused on attracting customers and consumers, it also works in solving employee needs.** The DuPont Corporation responded to the needs of its Wilmington, Delaware, employees by renovating a facility for daycare. Then they turned it over to the local YMCA, whose expertise qualified it as the logical manager. The results: a win-win solution for employees, employer, and the YMCA.

■ **Finding the right not-for-profit partner requires homework.** A good starting place is the local chapter of the National Society of Fund Raising Executives, or NSFRE's national headquarters at Alexandria, Virginia. You should also check your local Better Business Bureau to find out if they have received complaints about any charities. I would also recommend confirming that the not-for-profit you've chosen is, in fact, classified as such by the Internal Revenue Service. Donations are only deductible to 501(c)3 organizations.

GUIDELINES FOR CAUSE-RELATED MARKETING

Here are nine suggestions for businesses and charities considering participation in joint-venture marketing, as developed by the Council of the Better Business Bureau's Philanthropic Advisory Service:

1) Is the charity familiar with the participating corporation's subsidiaries, products and/or services?

2) Is the corporation informed about the participating charity's programs, finances, and other fund raising efforts?

3) Is there a written agreement that gives formal permission for the corporation to use the charity's name and logo?

4) Does the written agreement: (a) give the charity prior review and approval of ad materials that use its name, (b) indicate how long the campaign will last, (c) specify how and when charitable funds will be distributed, (d) explain any steps that will be taken in case of a disagreement or unforeseen result with the promotion?

5) Do the joint-venture advertisements: (a) specify the actual or anticipated portion of the sales or service price to benefit the charity, (b) indicate the full name of the charity, (c) include an address or phone number to contact for additional information about the charity or the campaign, (d) indicate when the campaign will end and, if applicable, the maximum amount the charity will receive?

6) Does the promotion follow all applicable state regulations in the areas the marketing will take place? Some states now have specific guidelines for sales made in conjunction with charities.

7) Does the corporation have fiscal controls in place to process and record the monies received to benefit the charity?

8) Will more than one charity be involved in the promotion? If so, how will funds be distributed?

9) Will the corporation complete a financial report at the end of the campaign (or annually, if the campaign lasts more than a year), which identifies (a) the total amount collected for the charity, (b) any campaign expenses, and (c) how much the charity received?

Cause-related marketing partnerships can be a golden opportunity for both partners. "Many nonprofits are sitting on their own undervalued assets," says Alan Toman, president of Marketing Department, Inc., a New York-based firm that specializes in helping to bring corporations and not-for-profits together in marketing arrangements. He is convinced that not-for-profits can offer highly targeted, segmented ways to reach key population groups.

"Nonprofits know the market extremely well. Their participation gives the company the equivalent of a Good Housekeeping Seal of Approval."

Part V

KEEPING YOUR BUSINESS
HEALTHY IN THE 1990s

Now we turn away from marketing, and concentrate on how demographics and psychographics will shape who runs and who works in this decade's businesses. We'll explore the trend towards smaller, more entrepreneurial businesses, a trend which continues to grow at the expense, perhaps, of corporate America. We'll look at the factors which point to a worker shortage in the decade ahead and into the twenty-first century.

Finally, we end our journey by returning to the predictions of Chapter 10, and looking ahead more generally and philosophically to what will drive our society as we begin a new century.

CHAPTER TWENTY

The Demographics of Leadership

IN THE 1990s, THE FASTEST GROWING BUSINESSES ARE NOT CORPORATIONS

The "under 100" list is where the action is. Here are some impressive statistics:

- Between 1978 and 1980, for the first time in America's history, self-employment in the U.S. grew at a faster rate than wage- and salary-paying jobs. By the mid-1980s, it was an "entrepreneurial explosion."

- At the forefront of the "explosion": women. Dun & Bradstreet reported more than 700,000 new business incorporations in the U.S. in 1987, plus another 250,000 unincorporated ventures. Of these, one-fourth are owned by females. "By the year 2000, we're projecting that as many as one-half of all sole proprietorships will be owned by women."*

- A growing phenomena are new-style "mom and pop" businesses. The Small Business Adminis-

---

*According to Carol Crockett, director of the Office of Women's Business Ownership, in Washington, D.C., a branch of the U.S. Small Business Administration.

tration says that between 1980 and 1986 (the last year for which statistics have been tabulated), the number of unincorporated businesses operated jointly—mainly by husbands and wives—increased by 62.7 percent. Some experts believe such businesses account for at least 1.5 million enterprises.

■ In the five year period from 1977 to 1982, the number of Hispanic businesses jumped from 220,000 to 400,000, an increase of 180 percent. The revenue from Hispanic businesses in 1982 was estimated at $20 million.

Why the growth? Pure demographics.

■ **The baby boomers are enthusiastic entrepreneurs.** Members of the baby boom generation are "clearly entrepreneurially inclined, excited by the romance of going into business for themselves."* Their interest has fueled the growth of such magazines as *Inc.* and *Entrepreneur.*

Boomers value entrepreneurship over climbing the corporate career ladder. Their hero may be Steve Jobs, the co-founder of Apple Computers. He made a fortune with personal computers, and then was forced to resign when he made moves to start a whole new enterprise, Next, Inc. "It's the idea that you can do it in the garage and wag your finger at IBM and get away with it," says Landon Jones. "And then when the company gets too institutionalized and oppressive, you start over."

Boomers may be looking at smaller, self-owned businesses as an alternative to the crowded path to the top of corporations. With competition so fierce from peers for a limited number of key positions, boomers are opting out in increasing numbers.

"We have a lot less loyalty to companies, and we put up with a lot less than our parents," concedes Rick Garnitz, 37,

---

*Leon Danco, president of the Center for Family Business, an educational and consulting firm in Cleveland.

who quit his job as a marketing manager at Xerox to start his own life-planning firm in Atlanta.

● **Family togetherness, a boomer value, is a renewed priority.** "Many couples are seeking ways to integrate their work life and their home life," says Sharon Nelton.* Combining work and leisure whenever possible is a unique characteristic of boomers.

Rebecca (35) and Dan (45) Matthias decided to run a business together even *before* they were married. "I think we discussed it on our first date," says Rebecca. By their second anniversary, she and Dan had launched Mothers Work Inc., a Philadelphia manufacturer and retailer of maternity clothes which cater to today's working woman. The company, fueled by boomer women demands, now has sales of $8 million.

■ **Hispanic business owners are responsive to markets ignored by more established corporations.** Although a handful of companies such as Anheuser-Busch, Coca-Cola, Kraft, and Campbell Soup have made special efforts to sell to the New America, big business still largely ignores it. Because success often requires comfort and familiarity with cultural differences, Hispanic entrepreneurs often do better within regional and local niches. For example: Hispanics spend relatively more of their free time with their extended families, so shopping is often a group affair requiring salespeople to accept a longer decision-making time. Product preference is often different, determined by tradition/brand loyalty and national reputation. Stores may need to be more gaily decorated.

● **Small business ownership is more comfortable for many Hispanics** who often find the corporate world filled with "people you are not familiar with, customers you're not familiar with. The corporation is big and complex. It can be very intimidating." Fernando Rios, a Pacific Bell Directory executive from East Los Angeles, find that a lot of Hispanics wind up in their own businesses. "It's a matter of access. When you run

---

*A family business expert at the U.S. Chamber of Commerce and author of *In Love and in Business*, a study of entrepreneurial couples.

your own business, your hard work and extra effort are rewarded much faster than in the corporate world."

■ **Older Americans are viewing retirement as a beginning, not an end.** Increasing life expectancy and better health among our older population are altering the very definitions of "old age" and "retirement." Mature Americans both need and want to work. They are attracted to the flexibility and challenge of starting their own businesses. A successful business is also a way to supplement a fixed income, and keep up with spiraling inflation.

And sometimes just the pure satisfaction of starting and operating a going concern is reason enough. Financial planner Chuck Jones asks, "Did Colonel Sanders really need the money when he started Kentucky Fried Chicken in his sixties?"

■ **Changing attitudes are also propelling women into the ranks of business owners.** Today, women are better educated and more business-oriented than ever. The "glass ceiling" stopping such women from attaining higher ranks in corporations causes many talented female executives to simply bypass the frustrations of corporate life by leaving the system and going into business for themselves.

According to the U.S. Small Business Administration, women are opening businesses at twice the rate of men. And a recent survey by Women in Franchising (WIF), a Chicago-based education firm that teaches women how to enter franchising, reveals that women, either alone or in partnership with men, own 30 percent of the nation's franchised businesses.

According to the *Avon Report*, a survey of 450 businesswomen, the most common reasons cited by women for starting their own businesses are: career control, opportunity, economic necessity, personal/family crisis, job dissatisfaction, greater dollars.

That view also shows up in a survey by Robert Hisrich, professor of business at the University of Tulsa, and Candida

Brush, a graduate business student at Boston University, who interviewed 344 women business owners for their 1986 book, *The Woman Entrepreneur*. Asked why they decided to found their own firms, many of the women said corporations still offer few opportunities for women to advance beyond middle management. Observes Katherine Bulow, former Assistant Secretary for Administration at the Department of Commerce: "Women get to a certain point and feel that they are not going any further. They take what they have learned and set up their own firms."

More women are prepared to run companies than ever before, since millions of them have landed professional jobs in fields that were once male dominated. And the most ambitious women, like their male counterparts, are no longer content to work for someone else, when rewards for striking out on their own can be much higher. Says Charlotte Taylor, president of Venture Concepts, a Washington consulting firm: "Women have gotten deadly serious about business ownership, not only as a career option but as a wealth-generating option. They are approaching it with exactly the same reasons and rationale that men do."

Women now constitute 27 percent of business owners. And women entrepreneurs are opening more businesses than ever before. In 1982 alone, 20 percent of all women started their own businesses. Women business owners are also younger. Fully 53 percent are younger than age 45. Robert Schwartz, who founded an "entrepreneur school" in Tarrytown, New York, in the mid 1970s, notes that women originally made up 5 to 10 percent of the classes. Now they're 50 percent.

Dun & Bradstreet Corporation, reporting on the more than 700,000 new-business incorporations in the United States in 1987, plus another 250,000 unincorporated ventures, noted that one-fourth are owned by females. Recent statistics show that women are initiating small-business start-ups at three times the rate of men, and thus comprise the fastest-growing segment of the self-employed community. Accordingly, Internal Revenue Service figures indicate that between 1980 and 1984, the number of female-owned sole proprietorships increased by 33 percent, while their sales receipts grew 54 percent. In 1987, there were 3.7 million female-owned proprietorships, up from 3.4 million in 1984, and their total sales receipts rose from $56 billion to $65 billion.

For other women, small business ownership solves the problems of combining family responsibilities with income needs. Sixty-three percent of today's female business owners have home-based operations—helped along by the technological advances of our age, and the accompanying affordability and accessibility of communication tools such as personal computers and mobile telephones.

MEANWHILE, BACK AT CORPORATE AMERICA

■ **Heading for the corner office: baby boomers.** During the 1990s, baby boomers will take over the leadership of corporate America. According to *Business Week*, the typical CEO of America's largest companies takes power at age 51. That means that by the year 2000, CEOs of even the biggest, most conservative companies will be drawn from the ranks of the postwar baby boom.

What changes can we expect? According to Richard Easterlin, of the University of Southern California, boomers are "a generation that carries the scars of its heritage."

The current chief executives who were born during the low-fertility years of the 1930s, and came of age during the post-World War II economic boom "... were the beneficiaries of a highly favorable combination of high demand for labor and labor-supply shortages. It was a generation that reached the top fairly easily."

Baby boomers, on the other hand, have fought for recognition and resources every step of the way. From overflowing classrooms in the 1950s to a tough labor market in the 1970s, brought up in the shadows of the Holocaust, the Bomb, and the Cold War, boomers tend to worry more and be more anxious about future security, according to Easterlin.

Even those boomers who chose business school during the Woodstock era emerged differently. Robert L. Virgil, dean of the John M. Olin School of Business at Washington University, says MBA classes of the years 1971 through 1975 were different from their predecessors. "Those students came through a tough period—social revolution, Vietnam," he says. "Their politics were more liberal, their social consciousness different."

Virgil notes that school was changing as well. Women and minorities were appearing in the classroom. That contributed to making students "more sensitized, more tolerant, more open to people of different backgrounds, races, and sex being on the management team." It also set the stage for women and minorities entering the ranks of CEOs of major companies by the year 2000.

Business Week suggests that, although the MBA graduates of the early 1970s did not embrace the alternative lifestyle of many of their peers, they were affected. "Some argue that these business leaders will be more loyal to companies and more appreciative of leisure and family. Their views on environmental issues will differ from those of earlier generations. "In addition, this will be the first generation of executives to feel comfortable dealing with computers and other information tools. *Business Week* also quotes Drexel University sociologist Arthur B. Shotak: "They will be more confident, more thick skinned, and more outspoken than previous executives."

Recognizing that the company of the future will be more complex, diverse and geographically spread out, these leadership qualities may, in fact, be just what tomorrow's baby boomer CEOs will need. According to Columbia University business school Professor Donald C. Hambrick, today's CEOs feel their successors will need to be charismatic to hold tomorrow's corporations together.

■ **Within the next five years, women will get to the corporate top,** suggests Lester Korn, chairman and cofounder of Korn/Ferry International, the world's largest executive-recruitment firm. He notes that "surveys show that a majority of all senior male executives really don't want the top job in their companies. But there certainly are a lot of women who do."

In an interview with Frances Lear, founder and editor of *Lear's* magazine, Korn asserts that women are "competing head-on with men, and they're winning. They're convincing the people who run corporate America that dealing with women in top positions is fine—which, I think, is the last barrier they face."

While he agrees that there's no question that women, especially older women, have great success when they go to work in small companies, or start companies of their own, Korn notes that women are in a better position "to take a crack at the top."

> You know, in 1986, at UCLA, we did a survey of the top 1,300 executives in corporate America. A handful were women. We did the same survey within the last year. We haven't released it yet, but I can tell you the percentage hasn't changed dramatically. Women are still not well represented at the top. But I believe they're going to get there. It's a matter of simple arithmetic: Just below the top 1,300 there's a stratum that's half women. Another helpful factor: Women on corporate boards are becoming more verbal about hiring and promoting women managers. We went through a phase in which boards of directors wanted a woman or two women. And they got them. In 59 percent of corporate America there's at least one woman on the board, and she's taking a much more active role than she did even five years ago, in terms of serving to prod management to bring women along. Not that she needs to prod very hard.

John Naisbitt and Patricia Aburdene concur. They call the '90s the "decade of women in leadership."

■ **Hispanics are not making it in corporate America,** according to an article in *California Business*. The problem, writer Dan Cook asserts, is not simply one of racism. There are few role models, few means by which even ambitious Hispanics can rise. They often choose to run their own businesses because they are intimidated by lack of access to the corporate "club." Organizations like the National Society of Hispanic MBAs have been formed to provide guidance and a network—a "club" of their own.

■ **Will an aging America accept older leadership?** The signs show that mandatory retirement and the automatic easing of older leaders out to pasture is being rethought. However, the deep distrust our society has for older persons is not likely to reverse dramatically now; rather, we should see changes when the boomers reach their sixties and seventies.

Who provides leadership to the businesses of the 1990s is only half the story; in Chapter 21 we'll discuss whom the employees of the 1990s are likely to be, and how to attract and retain them.

CHAPTER TWENTY-ONE

Attracting and Retaining Employees in the 1990s

CHANGING DEMOGRAPHICS WILL affect more than who your new customers are and how you'll reach them. There will also be a serious impact on who's available to work.

THE 1990s: A WORKER'S MARKET

"The 1990s may be the decade of the worker, as employers scramble to get and keep the best employees," according to *The Numbers News.*

Worker shortages will occur for three primary reasons:

- a dramatic decline in the available pool of traditional, entry-level workers

- a restructuring of the skills required in tomorrow's workplace

- an increasing demand for college-educated workers

■ **As the baby boom gives way to the baby bust,** "it won't be Business as Usual." Here's why, according to *Working Woman* magazine:

Not long ago, hiring new employees was easy. The baby boom had generated a long line of applicants for every opening. Choosing among excellent candidates was the most difficult part of the hiring process.

But this has changed drastically. The United States is facing its first labor shortage in 20 years. Unemployment is at its lowest point in 15 years—5.2 percent. And the tiny baby-bust generation, those born between 1964 and 1975, can't possibly fill all the entry-level positions the baby boom is vacating, or the millions of new jobs created each year. By 1990, the number of 18-year-olds will drop by 8 percent, according to a Census Bureau estimate, and will not reach 1989's level again until 2003.

Because we're facing a mere 1 percent a year workforce growth in the 1990s (compared to the vigorous 2.9 percent growth in the 1970s), the number of traditional entry-level workers will decline by a startling 20 to 25 percent!

Those industries which have relied on low-skilled, low-paid labor are already being affected. Industries that traditionally hire a lot of 18-year-olds—hotels, restaurants, banks, and insurance companies—are already scrambling for employees. "The first people to feel the labor crunch are those who have to hire the youngest people: McDonald's, K-mart," notes economist Richard Curtin, a director at the University of Michigan's respected Survey Research Center.

■ **The jobs themselves are becoming more demanding, more complex.** While computer technology and automation have taken the physical strain and boredom out of many jobs, work has become far more mentally demanding. Workers must handle a variety of skills, make snap decisions and adapt to unpredictable changes. The *Wall Street Journal* calls this "the workplace revolution" and notes that "the new jobs involve wrenching adjustments for both managers and workers. Managers who must delegate more decision-making feel threatened about relinquishing their power. Among workers, problem solving, analytical skills and teamwork are in high demand—and short supply."

The Hudson Institute, in a study for the Department of Labor called Workforce 2000, confirms the growing complexity of most jobs. By the year 2000, below-average skills will be good enough for only 27 percent of the jobs created between 1985 and 2000, compared with 40 percent of the jobs existing in the mid-1980s. And 41 percent of the new jobs will require average or better skill levels, up from 24 percent, the study says.

■ **The demand for college-educated workers may outstrip the supply in the 1990s.** The United States could experience labor shortages in occupational fields which require workers with postsecondary education. The U.S. Department of Labor, in a report on the employment outlook from 1988 to 2000, notes it expects the number of jobs requiring education beyond high school to rise 22 percent, compared with an overall job growth rate of 15 percent.

There could be trouble ahead for employers seeking natural scientists and engineers, for example, unless more women and minorities are attracted to these fields. Other fields for which shortages are expected: nurses, skilled craftsmen, computer wizards, retail workers, entertainers, lawyers and paralegals, and secretaries.

THE DEMOGRAPHICS OF THE WORKFORCE OF THE 1990s

More and more employers are competing for the best of the workforce pool: a pool that is both changing and shrinking.

■ **Women, older workers, minorities, new immigrants, the handicapped, and the disabled will, of necessity, find employers more welcoming.** "In today's economy, employers can't afford to discriminate," says Secretary of Labor Elizabeth Dole, who sees the shortage of workers as an "opportunity to assist those who have been at the end of the line for far too long."

Who will be applying for jobs in the 1990s? On average, 51 out of every 100 job applicants will be women, 77 will be

age 16 to 29, 15 will be Hispanics, 13 will be non-Hispanic blacks, and 6 will be Asians.

From now until the end of the century, 88 percent of workforce growth will come from women and minorities. White males, meanwhile, account for most retirees, and are leaving the workforce in record numbers. By the year 2000, white males, once the mainstay of the U.S. economy, will account for only 15 percent of new job recruits. Women will comprise two-thirds of the new workers and an additional 20 percent will be nonwhite or immigrant men.

"Now for every ten jobs there may be eight applicants. Four are women, and three are immigrants. Of the four young men applying, only two are white, and one may take drugs," notes Audrey Freedman, an economist at the Conference Board in New York.

BUILDING EMPLOYEE LOYALTY

Keeping productive employees should be a top concern for corporations, considering the fact that the average American worker has held eight jobs by the age of 40, according to a study released by Western U.S. Lifesaving Association.

A new Gallup survey shows that members of the post-war generations (baby boomers and baby busters) who entered the workforce since the 1960s are significantly less satisfied with their jobs than older Americans. Whereas only one in four (24 percent) workers between the ages of 18 and 49 are completely satisfied with their jobs, the rate of comparable satisfaction among older workers is nearly double.

■ **Marketing your business to potential workers is the key to surviving the worker shortage,** says John Mancuso, a senior consultant at the Wyatt Company's Boston office. "Anyone can put a help-wanted ad in a newspaper." But to compete effectively against other businesses, "employers must evaluate what benefits appeal to their target labor pool, and then find cost-effective ways to offer these benefits."

■ **Providing Employee Assistance Programs that resolve problems** can keep a valued employee on the job. EAPS can offer a wide range of services to achieve the goal of maintaining fully productive employees. Today such programs range from encouraging workers to stay healthy by providing fitness programs at the workplace (over half of businesses with 50 or more employees have at least one health promotion program, according to a nationwide study of 1,358 businesses done in January 1989), to providing or identifying services for resolving problems with substance abuse, child and elder care, family conflict, finances, legal matters, and organizational conflict.

Tuition-assistance programs, job sharing, employee savings plans, and four-day workweeks are some of the "bells and whistles" employers should consider, says Mancuso.

● **Childcare: the outstanding employee benefit of the nineties.** Economists see the general tightening of the labor market as the century draws to a close as a boon to working mothers. The competition for talented workers will not only force employers to compete for the services of working mothers, but will force companies to lure nonworking mothers into the market.

In a world where most women work, the separation between work life and home life has become less distinct. Problems once handled at home are invading the workplace, because there may be no one at home to deal with the problems. Companies will be under greater pressure to offer daycare benefits, as well as part-time and flextime hours, to attract and retain women as well as men.

Those industries which require highly skilled, highly trained professionals are likely to respond first. If women lawyers or nurses gravitate towards firms and hospitals where time out for babies or part-time work does not foreclose the possibility of their advancement, other firms and hospitals will have to follow suit.

"Despite the rapid entry of women with young children into the labor force, many mothers are still prevented from working by scarcity and high cost of quality child care. Employers are beginning to see the link between child care initiatives and bottom-line profitability. The stage is definitely set for child care to become the fringe benefit of the 1990s," notes

David Bloom, Ph. D., professor of economics at Columbia University.

Felice Schwartz* agrees. She believes that in the 1990s, companies which are reluctant to work with women (and men) on daycare issues may find themselves short of help. "The days of considering women superfluous are over," says Schwartz; companies no longer have the luxury of giving hiring and promotion preferences to men because they don't take maternity leaves.

Thus, according to Martin O'Connell, of the Census Bureau, employers "will have an incentive to understand and cater to the special needs of working mothers."

Eventually, the need to attract and retain valuable workers will force employers to restructure the workplace to be more consonant with the requirements of women with young children. By choosing to work in what Sheila Kamerman, Ph.D., and her collaborator Alfred Kahn, Ph.D.,[†] call "the responsive workplace," and choosing not to work in an unresponsive workplace, women can spark a real change in society.

What percentage of mothers of young children are in the labor force? Overall, sixty-five percent of all mothers with children under 18 work.

Fifty-six percent of those with children under six work. Percentages by the age of the child are:

Age of child (years)	Mothers in the workforce(%)
1 year or younger	50.8
2	60.3
3	59.3
4	61.3
5	63.6

It makes sense that "corporations are rethinking the relationship between work life and home life, recognizing that work and family can no longer be considered separate."**

---

*Founder of Catalyst, a New York-based research organization that studies issues affecting women's careers.

†Professors of Social Policy and Planning at the Columbia University School of Social Work.

**Barbara Adolf, author of The Employer's Guide to Child Care.

Dana Friedman and Wendy Gray suggest a truly "family-oriented approach," noting that critical events in employees' lives—being hired, getting married, having and raising children, getting divorced, retiring, and dying—are characterized by unique needs that can be served by offering a menu of financial assistance, services, counseling, and schedule flexibility.* For example, prenatal care is an increasingly popular benefit, one which can reduce the risks of costly premature births, resulting in "healthy babies, happy parents, and reasonable medical bills."

Joan Beck, a columnist for the *Chicago Tribune*, reports that "some of the nation's best-managed, most successful, and most innovative corporations are experimenting with new ways to attract and hold non-traditional workers, especially mothers trying to balance home responsibilities with paying jobs."

Beck's article cites the October 1989 issue of *Working Mother* magazine, which salutes 60 companies that offer innovative help to employees with family concerns. What forms does help take?

Most of the companies offer some help with daycare. The easiest are referral services and pretax salary set-asides employees can use to pay for daycare.

Some companies go much further. A growing number of corporations—Apple Computers, Campbell Soup, Champion International, Dominion Bankshares, FirstAtlanta, Hoffman-LaRochre, and StrideRite, for example—provide daycare facilities in their own headquarters. American Bankers Insurance Group also offers an on-site public school for primary grades.

DuPont, Dow Chemical, and Proctor & Gamble, among others, give substantial funding to child-care facilities in the community that their employees can use. Polaroid subsidizes daycare on a sliding scale for lower-income employees. Aetna Life & Casualty finances some training for daycare providers.

Arthur Andersen operates a Saturday daycare center for employees during its busy tax season. Some divisions of Time Inc. furnish emergency back-up care. And Fel-Pro not only offers on-site daycare, but a summer day camp program, and pro-

---

*Conference Board report, "A Life Cycle Approach to Family Benefits and Policies."

vides at-home tutoring for employees' children with learning problems.

A large majority of these highly rated employers allow employees to work flexible hours, and most approve job-sharing arrangements and/or provide part-time work. A few—Johnson & Johnson, IBM, Merck, the law firm Morrison & Foerster, Time Inc. and US West, among others—let some employees work at home.

Concludes Beck, "...All of these innovative work patterns can be cost-effective for employers, particularly because they cut employee turnover, reduce absenteeism, lessen stress and help recruit the best workers."

● **Eldercare: the growing concern for the future.** Elder care may be the concern of the future, suggests Ken Dychtwald. Your older workers may need help with spouses, and your boomer and female workers may be handling parental and grandparent's care.

In 1989, *Fortune* magazine and John Hancock Financial Services undertook to assess how corporate executives and employees in America are dealing with elder care issues. They found that the vast majority (89 percent) of corporate executives consider health care for the elderly to be a major problem in the United States. This viewpoint is similarly held by the employees surveyed (94 percent).

In a special issue dealing with the 1990 outlook, *US News & World Report* warns of an impending "elder-care crisis"; since the parents of most people now in the work force are still too young to need daily assistance, most companies have not yet felt the disruptive effects of an aging and longer-lived population on their employees.

The *Fortune*/John Hancock survey suggests corporate executives are already cognizant of the effect that employee elder care is having on the workplace. Six out of ten (60 percent) of the executives surveyed are aware of specific work-related problems. The predominant problems are employee stress (45 percent), unscheduled days off (38 percent), late arrivals and early departures (37 percent), above-average use of the telephone (32 percent), and absenteeism. Those in service companies are more likely than those in industrial companies to report having these problems.

Consultant Fran Sussner Rodgers* agrees. Companies grappling with elder care will probably focus initially on such referral networks, since elder care is complicated by distance. More than half of the 12,000 or so employees of companies Rodgers has worked with lived more than 100 miles from elderly dependents. "Crises are common," she says. Perhaps an elderly parent must be hospitalized unexpectedly, and then comes home too weak to recover without help. Or siblings scattered in several states must instantly compare resources in their communities to determine where an ailing parent should move.

Other kinds of company policies or programs that are currently available to help employees deal with taking care of elderly relatives or friends include personal days off, health benefits coverage for family members, unpaid leaves of absence, and sick days. Employee assistance programs (EAPS) that offer elder care service guidance, information and referral on elderly services, and flexible benefit plans with Dependent Care Assistance (DCAP) are less widely available. Many companies contribute to community aging programs as well.

A few companies, such as the Travelers Companies and IBM, are in the forefront of corporate America's efforts to address the issue. They have surveyed their employees' needs, and responded with assistance aimed at reducing the emotional stress, physical demands, and cost of caring for an older relative. "While elder-care policies are too new for us to prove that their bottomline impact compares to that of progressive child-care and maternity-leave policies, the aging of the population guarantees that elder care is the new frontier of corporate benefits."†

● **Helping the "sandwiched" employee.** Five million Americans (typically, a female age 53, but increasingly a baby boomer) can already be classified as members of the "sand-

---

*Her firm, Work/Family Directions in Watertown, Massachusetts, sets up information networks for her clients to refer employees to child care and elder care in their community.

†Frances R. Rothstein, writing in *Working Woman*.

wich generation," caught in the squeeze between caring for children and dependent parents. Numbers are increasing steadily as medical technology keeps more Americans alive longer.

For women handling the needs of an aging parent or parent-in-law, in addition to caring for children, the strain can be terrible. Many switch to part-time jobs, pass up promotions, or quit their jobs altogether.

Dr. Michael Creedon* has developed an intergenerational daycare program now in place at Stride-Rite and ten other companies. Most of the intergenerational daycare programs focus on providing care to old and young in one place, thus easing the burden for the middle-aged adult who would otherwise shuttle between children and parents.

■ **Use community outreach and employee volunteerism to help build employee loyalty.** The Chivas Regal Report on Working Americans indicates that corporate involvement in public service makes a difference: 45 percent of workers surveyed say their loyalty would increase if their corporations were involved in public service activities. Even among those who say their loyalty has decreased in recent years, a significant number (37 percent) say they would feel more loyal if they knew about charitable contributions or public service activities of their company. Other research has found that companies exhibiting social consciousness perform better financially when compared to companies that are involved less with social issues!

Perhaps unexpectedly, upscale **baby boomers**—the high educated, high income "Yuppie" your company wants to retain—wants to contribute to the public good. One in three (33 percent) of this group says the desire to contribute to society is a key priority for them, compared with 15 percent of other working Americans.

● **Reward employee volunteerism, and you'll build employee loyalty.** "Some companies, such as Xerox and Wells Fargo, offer employees paid community-involvement sabbaticals, during which they can work with not-for-profit agencies.

---

*Director of corporate programs at the National Council on Aging.

At Xerox, employees can take up to a year at full pay and bene-fits; at Wells Fargo, they can take up to six months. Recently, a senior systems analyst at Wells Fargo took six months off to or-ganize and promote recreational programs for disabled people; a project manager helped a child-abuse prevention program develop drop-in centers; and an assistant vice-president devel-oped a countrywide organ-donor awareness program,'' reports Ken Dychtwald.

While Americans volunteer for a wide variety of public is-sues and institutions, four issues top the list of problems about which they are most especially concerned. Large numbers of working Americans says they are personally distressed about the drug problem (55 percent), AIDS (49 percent), environ-mental pollution (40 percent), the quality of public education (39 percent), and the plight of the homeless (33 percent). And well over half the working population (58 percent) say they would be willing to volunteer time to help resolve some of these problems.*

Specific Demographic Keys to Attracting Employees

■ **Boomer-oriented?** Here are some suggestions:

● **Make your working conditions attractive.** Follow this check list.

- Are your hours flexible?

- Do you provide valued employees with a physical place of their own which they can decorate?

- Does the cafeteria serve food and drink that fits their lifestyle—decaffeinated coffee, herbal tea, yogurt, mineral water, etc.?

- Do you use lush plants and bold graphics to provide an atmosphere that parallels their own homes?

*The Chivas Regal Report on Working Americans

● **Provide instant gratification.** Boomers need lots of appreciation. Let them know when they've done the job well. Constant, small pats on the back are better than a yearly review. They especially like tangible rewards: a letter for their personnel file, a certificate of appreciation, and, of course, salary reviews.

■ **Want to attract Hispanic Americans?** Cultural differences make recruitment of Hispanic Americans difficult for non-Hispanic management. The key is to learn what those differences are.

● **Consider recruiting Hispanics as groups, rather than as individuals.** Why? Because Hispanics families are frequently large and close-knit. Encourage all interested members of the family to come at one time and discuss the variety of positions available in your organization. Or, exhibit at a community job fair.

● **Involve the men first.** Why? Because men tend to dominate Hispanic households. Their permission is often necessary before the rest of the family can participate. And be aware that Hispanic families take the safety and respect accorded to unmarried Hispanic women very seriously.

● **Make your organization look friendly and familiar.** Have a fluent Spanish-speaking manager available at all times. Try to incorporate Latin music, brighter colors, and bolder graphics into your ambiance.

● **Respond to their sense of family.** Invite family members to your company events. Make sure to publicize staff accomplishments in the local Hispanic media as well as general publications.

● **Recruit visibly and actively.** Recruit in both Spanish and English. Use direct mail with coupons for responses. Offer tapes and reprints of articles about your company both in Spanish and English.

■ **Older workers can be a boon to your organization.** President George Bush put it this way: "We must bring in the generations, harnessing the unused talent of the elderly."

You can benefit by making use of their well-honed skills and their reliability. Many businesses are already marketing job positions to older Americans, inviting them to consider flexible or reduced hours.

McDonald's has been running commercials, aptly titled "New Kid on the Block," suggesting retired individuals consider the positive rewards—companionship, respect, and good pay—waiting at McDonald's.

But you've got to be sensitive to the needs and feelings of these older workers. For example, contrary to what most younger people think, they don't see themselves as having "all the time in the world." They may only have a few good years left, and they will be careful how they spend them. But many older persons want to stay busy. They don't see retirement as days and nights before the television. They want to continue to learn and to have new and meaningful experiences. Recruit at senior citizen groups, service clubs, pre-retirement workshops, and through your current older workers.

● **Make older workers a part of your organization.** Even if they work part-time, give them their own spot. Invite them to contribute to the company newsletter and to join the company sports teams; introduce them to new employees, and ask their advice.

● **Let them do something "different" if they want to.** When you retire in your late fifties or early sixties, you've spent a lot of time in a career. If older workers want to use their skills differently—or develop totally new skills—respect their wishes. On the other hand, often an older professional person—an accountant or an attorney, for example—doesn't want to lose the network he or she has built up. A consulting arrangement may be appealing.

● **Watch your physical facilities.** Don't force older workers to climb mile-long staircases, fight off muggers on the way in your front door, or walk unnecessary distances between the

Courtesy of American Protective Servicesinc., Vancouver, Washington

parking lot and the building. In short, remember their physical limitations.

● **Offer them the "golden benefit" of health care coverage.** This is an important real income supplement which can entice retirees back to work.

■ **Interested in recruiting women workers?** Many companies are using magazines like *Working Woman, Savvy,* and *Working Mother* to target career-oriented women.

● **Search where talented women abound.** Use word-of-mouth in the right places to let people know you're looking. Introduce your cause and yourself to women at meetings of professional women's groups and mixed-sex luncheons. Look in professional publications, in business publications, and alumnae magazines for promotions: write notes of congratulation and mention you're searching for talented employees.

● **Be alert to safety.** It's not discriminatory to be concerned for a woman's safety. Review your facilities and eliminate situations where women are apt to be mugged or sexually attacked.

<hr>

VALUING DIVERSITY

For many companies, the problem is not getting minorities and women in the door. It is keeping them. The crucial questions for the employer and his/her human resources manager becomes how can we best manage, communicate, and work with people different from ourselves?

■ **Cultural diversity is a fact of life in today's—and tomorrow's—workplace.** Diversity can bring innovation, creativity, and better problem-solving. A culturally sensitive, diverse workforce enables organizations to better understand and serve its equally diverse customers and consumers. But the benefits are not automatic: tension among employees lowers productivity and creates high costs in employee absenteeism,

AT KELLY, THE WORKFORCE OF TOMORROW IS HERE TODAY

Women hold 85% of Kelly's management positions.

Twenty-five percent of our corporate officers are women.

Across America, women comprise more than 85% of our
total annual workforce of more than 560,000.

We developed our Displaced Homemakers and Single Parents program,
and our Working Solutions for Military Spouses program
to focus on the special needs of these working women.

We provide free training to more than 6,000 temporary employees
each week, offering our employees greater opportunities
to build skills and earn higher pay.

By the year 2000, the number of women entering the workforce will increase dramatically. At Kelly, we've already responded by creating an environment that meets the needs of working women today. Our strong commitment has enabled us to recruit and retain some of the best and brightest women from our nation's workforce.

We'll continue to meet the challenges of a changing workforce by offering better opportunities and greater flexibility in the workplace. Because at Kelly Services, with Kelly Temporary Services and Kelly Assisted Living, we recognize the importance of women in the future workforce and to the future of our company.

KELLY
SERVICES
The First and The Best®

©1989 Kelly Services, Inc.   Kelly Services, Inc. is an equal opportunity employer M/F/H/V   Not an agency · never a fee

Reprinted with permission of Kelly Services, Inc., Troy, Michigan.

turnover, EEO and harassment suits, and unrest. And failure to understand cultural differences can lead to misunderstandings, poor performance, and unwise hiring and firing decisions.

■ **Diversity has to be deliberately well managed.** The future success of American enterprise, in both the public and private sectors, will depend largely on how well employment and management policies accommodate a diverse labor pool. According to Xerox CEO David Kearns, "The company that gets out in front in managing diversity will have the competitive edge." Leading organizations concur:

- Dupont's *Diversity: A Source of Strength* report: "Strength gained from diversity is the goal of our affirmative action program...Diversity is inevitable. The vision is to manage this to our advantage."

- AT&T's 1988 forecast: "AT&T faces difficult transitions requiring a major rethinking of human resource management...It will be increasingly important not only to accommodate cultural and language differences, but to tap and mine those differences as important human resources."

- Hewlett-Packard's CEO John Young: "Our diverse workforce helps HP realize its full potential. Managers are responsible for creating a work environment to which the contributions of all people are recognized. To do this, they need to understand how best to utilize individual differences."

■ **Valuing diversity is a new concept, not merely new words for equal employment opportunities or affirmative action,** insists the wife/husband team of Lennie Copeland and Lewis Griggs.

They are producers of a three-part film/video series which shows specific situations which cause conflict and poor performance, and how such situations can be better handled. The series features individuals from Aetna, Avon Products, Bank of America, Booz Allen & Hamilton, Colgate-Palmolive, Hallmark Cards, Hewlett-Packard, Honeywell, Xerox, Stanford University, and the U.S. Department of Housing and Urban Development sharing their experiences and insights into the multicultural workplace.

> Valuing diversity means recognizing and appreciating that individuals are different, that diversity is an advantage if it is valued and well managed, and that diversity is not to be simply tolerated but encouraged, supported, and nurtured.
>
> Valuing diversity is a state that reflects a point of view, an attitude, a purpose, and actions that are essentially different from EEO and affirmative action. Valuing diversity looks at the multicultural workforce from a positive perspective, rather than a defensive position.

According to Copeland, many EEO and HRD professionals seem to agree that five major problem areas need attention:

- stereotypes and their associated assumptions

- actual cultural differences

- exclusivity of the "white male club," and its associated access to important information and relationships

- unwritten rules and double standards for success which are often unknown to women and minorities

- lack of communication about differences

The *Valuing Diversity* training materials assert that overcoming these barriers to valuing diversity requires specifically addressing each problem through a clear plan of action. Copeland says that managers need to:

- Recognize the assumptions they make and how these affect decisions; avoid letting stereotypes interfere with valid assessments and good judgment.

- Invite outsiders into the "club" and provide employees who are different with what they need to succeed: access to information and meaningful relationships with people in power.

- Teach the unwritten rules to those who need to know them. And change the rules when necessary to allow diversity to benefit the organization.

- Encourage constructive communication about differences.

- Treat people equitably but not uniformly. Build on individual differences. Value diversity.

■ **Move your organization towards the future, don't resist it.** As Xerox chairman David Kearns says, "Understand that over the long term, the successful manager is going to have a deal with large numbers of minorities and women in business, and I presume most managers want to be successful, want their company to be successful. Therefore, don't walk away from it; walk up to it."

CHAPTER TWENTY-TWO

Predicting the Future: Looking Ahead to the 21st Century

*T*HE FUTURE IS HERE—at least demographically. Almost all the people (over 80 percent) who will comprise the U.S. population in the year 2000 are alive. The Population Reference Bureau notes that "This means that the U.S. labor force of the next century is already born (although not necessarily all in the United States): next century's first high school graduating class (as well as its dropouts) are already in grade school; and the elderly of the 21st century are already well down paths that will determine their financial and health care needs for old age."

■ **The 1990s are a window of opportunity,** according to *America in the 21st Century: A Demographic Overview.** We can look ahead and prepare for the issues that are likely to confront us in the twenty-first century. What trends can we predict with a fair degree of certainty?

The demographic trends that will most significantly impact the social and economic development of our country in the next century are:

---

*Prepared by the Population Reference Bureau and the Population Resource Center, and sponsored by the Ford Foundation.

- The aging of the population

- Changes in our household and family structures

- Changes in our racial and ethnic composition

- Changes in our residential patterns

- Changes in the distribution of income and wealth

- Changes in our labor force needs

- The changing global demographic picture

■ **An aging nation** will find the strain of caring for the elderly growing. The fastest growing segment of the U.S. population is those 85+. By 2030, their numbers will triple. Those 85+ will greatly impact services for the elderly, and cause economic strain, as they are four times more likely than 65- to 74-year-olds to require long-term care services.

In addition, problems regarding the funding of Social Security will arise in the early part of the twenty-first century, when the baby boomers begin retiring; the baby busters are a much smaller population cohort. The aged dependency ratio (the number of elderly persons compared to all working persons, 18 to 64) is steadily increasing—in 1950 it was 13:100; today, 20:100; projected in 2030, 37:100. To compensate for the growing number of future elderly, Social Security has announced that in 2000, and continuing for 27 years, the age at which a person may retire with full Social Security benefits will rise from 65 to 67.

The aging of America raises three key policy issues:

- We will need to plan for and provide services to increasing numbers of older people, particularly those age 85 and over. Health care and retirement income programs will be most critically impacted by shifting demographic patterns.

- We will need to reformulate the level and kinds of investments that we make in our schools and job training programs. With fewer children in the population, schools will have an opportunity to reduce class size, and give more attention to individual students.

- We will need to rethink our policies regarding work and retirement, in order to accommodate our changing age structure and future labor force demands. Retraining (and retaining) older workers may become an economic necessity in the years ahead.

■ **Single parent households will be one-third of family structures.** Today less than 10 percent of households fit the traditional family model of the 1960s, with dad working, mom at home and three or more kids. By the end of the 1980s, the typical family was a one or two or no child household, with both parents working. Twenty-three percent of children under 18 lived in single parent homes. Nonfamily households—persons living alone or with unrelated individuals—had risen from 15 to 26 percent. By the year 2000, they'll rise to 32 percent.

The interaction between changing age structure and changing household and family patterns will influence the housing and labor markets of the next century in at least four ways, according to *America in the 21st Century*:

- We can expect a slower rate of growth in the housing market, at least among first-time home buyers, as the baby bust cohort replaces the baby boom cohort in the housing market. Whether this trend will reduce the demand for housing, thereby lowering prices and closing the affordability gap, remains to be seen. In the meantime, pressure will build on policy makers to take action on various housing initiatives (rent subsidies, housing vouchers, and tax programs) to reduce the cost of housing for low- and middle-income families.

- There will be greater segmentation within the housing market, reflecting the more complex and diverse lifestyles of American families. Smaller families, dual-earner couples, and elderly who live alone will place special demands on the nation's housing stock. Meeting the varied needs of distinct population groups will be a major challenge for the housing industry in the years ahead.

- The growing number of working parents will demand more flexibility at the work place. Many businesses and corporations already are instituting flexible work schedules, part-time jobs, and shared job arrangements that enable employees to fulfill their family obligations.

- Employers also will face increasing pressure to adjust their personnel policies and benefit programs to reflect changing family patterns. The growing concern over child care, elder care, and parental leave will continue well into the next century, as the middle-aged baby boom cohort copes with the responsibilities of rearing their children *and* caring for their aging parents.

■ **Immigration from other countries, and fertility rates at home, are changing the racial and ethnic composition of the United States.** By 2000, nearly one-third of all school age children will be from minority populations. Today, minorities account for about 20 percent of the U.S. population. This proportion will rise to almost one-third by 2030.

While blacks are still the dominant minority group in the U.S., representing about 60 percent of all minority people, Hispanics are the fastest growing segment of the minority population. Asians represent approximately 10 percent of U.S. minorities, but their numbers are expected to rise significantly.

The changing racial and ethnic composition of the U.S. will put increasing pressure on many of the basic institutions of our society, and challenge our fundamental beliefs in inclusion, acculturation, and nondiscrimination. The most visible changes should occur in five areas:

- School systems face the challenge of educating a more diverse population, in which many students enter the school system lacking basic English language and learning skills.

- States and municipalities will need to find ways of absorbing immigrant groups into their local economies. Public officials will face continuing concern over the effect of these new arrivals on the types and availability of jobs, wage rates, and social service needs.

- The court system will be asked to clarify or redefine such public policy areas as affirmative action and minority set-asides, as some segments of the minority population begin to compete more effectively within the existing economic system.

- Changing racial and ethnic patterns will noticeably affect political parties and the voting electorate. As minority populations become more active in the political process, they are likely to press for greater representation within all levels of government, and within political party structures.

- Immigration policies will continue to be debated, as American labor force needs and international events change over time. As in the past, the debate will focus on what criteria should be used for accepting new immigrants; the impact of illegal immigration on the economy; and the process by which new immigrants adjust to American lifestyles, and become productive members of society.

Source: *America in the 21st Century*

■ **By 2010, the majority (60 percent) of population will live in the South or the West.** California will remain the most populous state, but Texas will overtake New York for the number two position in the early 1990s. Florida will remain the fourth largest state, but by 2000, Illinois will replace Pennsylvania in fifth place. Between 1990 and 2000, nine states (eight in the South or West) will grow twice as fast as the nation as a whole, while 13 states (mainly in the Midwest farm belt) will lose population. Wyoming, Vermont and North Dakota will be the least populous states in the U.S.

New patterns of metropolitan growth are emerging with the rapid growth of new *outer cities*—employment and residential centers on the suburban fringes of major metropolitan areas—which are attracting a significant number of young families.

Changing residential patterns will play an increasingly important role in shaping not only our future political structures, but also the governance and management of the public sector. Notes *America in the 21st Century*, we can expect that:

- The sunbelt region of the country will continue to gain political clout as people continue to relocate to this area.

- The political strength of suburban areas and newly emerging urban areas will grow at the expense of older cities and rural areas.

- Changing residential patterns will challenge the ability of state and local governments to provide and maintain essential public services and in-

frastructure systems. The size and composition
of local communities will affect not only the demand for public services, but also the tax base
for financing these services.

- Regional advisory groups or governing bodies
  will become more prominent as problems associated with economic development and resource use cut across traditional political and
  jurisdictional boundaries. However, addressing
  these issues in a coordinated fashion may require a painful realignment of traditional lines
  of authority, funding arrangements, and mecha-
  nisms for accountability.

■ **The demographic composition of the poor is shifting.** While
the proportion of persons living in poverty has declined over
the past thirty years, the composition has changed dramatically. Whereas the elderly once had the highest rates of poverty
(one in three elderly were classified as poor in 1959), now persons living in female-headed households and people living
alone are at greatest risk of being poor. Today, only 12 percent
of all elderly persons are regarded as poor, but 20 percent of all
children live in poverty.

To break the cycle of poverty requires giving these younger
Americans socioeconomic mobility. Yet obtaining a good education or marketable skills, finding transportation to the areas
where jobs exist, or even developing relationships with successful role models have all become more problematic for people living in poverty areas, according to *America in the 21st
Century*.

To attack the problems of poverty and foster the means for
achieving upward mobility, the report recommends imple-
menting a broad range of policy options, among them:

- Programs that help young children get a better
  start on life—quality daycare and school enrich-
  ment programs—are essential components of
  such assistance.

- Programs that help pregnant teens prepare for their role as parents and assist them in completing school.

- Job training and job counseling programs that help unemployed or welfare-dependent people become self-supporting.

- Programs that help make housing more affordable, not only for first-time home buyers, but also for those who rent.

- A reappraisal of tax policies and income-generating plans that will enable government at the federal, state, and local levels to finance programs to assist persons in need.

■ **The composition of the work force is clearly changing, and so is the nature of the job market.** There appears to be a growing mismatch between workers' skills and job requirements. Workforce readiness, more than the actual size of the future labor force, will be the most troubling issue of the twenty-first century. If the United States is to continue to compete, our workforce will need to become more productive. Educators, policy makers, and employers, recommends *America in the 21st Century*, will have to keep a number of considerations in mind:

- Educators will have to integrate the need for student mastery of basic learning skills with reasoning. All levels of education will face a growing demand for higher performance standards.

- The concept of *life-long education* will gain greater prominence in the workplace. Workers of all ages and all levels will need to be retrained several times throughout their working life to keep pace with the changing demands of the future work environment.

- Employers will have to adopt more flexible work policies in order to recruit and retain future workers. With more women and older workers in tomorrow's workforce, policies such as child care, parental leave, flexible work hours, work at home, and pension portability will take on greater significance.

- Debate over U.S. immigration policies will continue as some employers seek to fill gaps in labor force supply with workers from abroad.

■ **Our prosperity will be intrinsically linked to the social and economic well-being of the world community.** While increased competition for product markets, labor markets, and investment markets is likely to intensify as each nation pursues its own economic agenda, opportunities for cooperative agreements and joint ventures may also be greater than ever before, suggests *America in the 21st Century*. The demographic trends that lie behind the shift to a global economy provide an important framework for understanding the issues and conflicts involved. We can expect that:

- Economic and trade policies will alternate between competition and cooperation with other countries of the world. Whether we institute trade barriers or launch joint ventures, we will need to plan long-range strategies for increasing the productivity and financial strength of American enterprise.

- Labor policies will choose among three distinct, but not mutually exclusive, alternatives: importing labor from abroad: training (or retraining) U.S. workers; or exporting jobs to countries with lower labor costs. U.S. policy debates on economic competition and changing labor force needs will hinge on the desirability and consequences of these options. Different industries or economic sectors will pursue different strategies, as no single policy will fit the circumstances of all.

- Greater emphasis will be placed on the potential environmental impact of foreign assistance programs as they promote modernization and expand economic development in the less developed regions of the world.

- International demographic and economic trends suggest that the U.S. may no longer dominate the world's social, political, and economic order as it did in the mid-20th century. Instead, U.S. foreign policy of the next century will increasingly have to recognize the need for regional balance, mutual cooperation, and global interdependency. Fostering a spirit of cooperation and reducing world tensions may be the most important leadership role the U.S. can play in the years ahead.

In conclusion

I deliberately moved this book away from its very pragmatic orientation to conclude with a broader picture of the future. As business persons and as marketers, we need to address specifics that impact on our day-to-day success; but each of us must also be aware of our opportunity to use the 1990s to set the stage for a new century. I am most appreciative of the work of the Population Reference Bureau and the Population Resource Center whose report, *America in the 21st Century*, provides a thoughtful and thought-provoking demographic overview of the future.

BIBLIOGRAPHY

Part 1

Chapter 1
Hodgkinson, Harold L. "Demography is Destiny." *CASE Currents*, July/August 1987.

Chapter 2
Original material from Daniel Hansler, Fund Raising Marketing Company, Concord, CA.

Chapter 3
Mitchell, Arnold. *The Nine American Lifestyles*. New York: Macmillan, 1983.

Mitchell, Arnold. "Styles in the American Bullring." *Across the Board*, March 1983.

Mills, D. Quinn. "How to Improve Your Marketing with Psychographics." Presented at American Demographics Conference, June 3, 1987.

Posner, Fred. "Focusing on the New 'Power Groups'." Presented at American Demographics Institute's Demographic Outlook '86 Conference, June 4, 1986.

The Influential Americans. 2d ed. New York: The Roper Organization, Inc., October 1988.

Kanner, Bernice. "Mind Games." *Best of Business Quarterly* 1989. (Reprinted from *New York Magazine*)

Nichols, Judith E. "How to Use Demographics and Psychographics to Build Your Donor Base." Presented at American Demographics Seminar, Target Marketing for Non-Profit Organizations. September 1988.

Chapter 4
"The Best 100 Sources for Marketing Information." *Who's Who from American Demographics*, January 1990.

Part 2

Farnsworth Riche, Martha. "Holistic Marketing." *American Demographics*, January 1990.

Chapter 5

Marinucci, Carla. "Baby Boomers Take Over." *San Francisco Examiner*, November 20, 1987.

Thomas, Evan. "Growing Pains at 40." *Time*, May 19, 1986.

Russell, Cheryl. "What's Going to Happen When the Baby Boom Gets Older." Presented at American Demographics Conference, June 3, 1987.

Jones, Landon Y. *Great Expectations*. New York: Ballantine Books, 1980.

"Meet the Would-Be's, a Mass Market Elite." *The Numbers News* 8, no. 7 (July 1988).

Russell, Cheryl. "No Sure Thing." *American Demographics*, July 1988.

Mills, American Demographics Conference, 1987.

Royer, Mary-Paige. "Please Give Generously, Okay?" *American Demographics*, June 1988.

Smith, Nancy. "In the Shadow of Boomers." The Oregonian, July 30, 1989.

"Moms pitch M.O.M." USA Today, March 8, 1989.

Rothenberg, Randall. "Nostalgia becomes a craze of the present." The Oregonian, December 10, 1989.

Chapter 6

Kotkin, Joel. "Selling to the New America." Inc., July 1987.

The Pocket Book of Hispanic Facts. Mt. Pleasant, Iowa: Alaniz & Sons, 1988.

Schwartz, Joe. "Hispanics in the Eighties." American Demographics, January 1988.

Francese, Peter. "Hispanic Population rising sharply in U.S." Detroit Free Press, March 1, 1987.

Farnsworth Riche, Martha. "California, Here It Comes." American Demographics, March 1989.

Lacayo, Richard. "A Latin Wave Hits the Mainstream." Time, July 11, 1988.

Schwartz, Joe. "Rising Status." American Demographics, January 1989.

"Hispanics in the Eighties." American Demographics, July 1988.

Greene, Stephen G. "The Challenge of Ethnic Diversity." Chronicle of Philanthropy, July 11, 1989.

Swenson, Chester A. "How to Speak to Hispanics." American Demographics, February 1990.

Chapter 7

Hunt, Ann. "The Over-50 Market." The Oregonian, April 14, 1988.

Jones, Landon Y. *Great Expectations.*

Edmondson, Brad. "Inside the Empty Nest." *American Demographics*, November, 1987.

Lazer, William and Eric H. Shaw. "How Older Americans Spend Their Money." *American Demographics*, September 1987.

Longino, Jr., Charles F. "The Comfortably Retired and the Pension Elite." *American Demographics*, June 1988.

Dychtwald, Ken and Joe Flower. *Agewave.* Los Angeles: Tarcher, 1989.

Ostroff, Jeff. "An Aging Market." *American Demographics*, May 1989.

Tobin, Thomas C. "A New Class of Seniors." *New Choices*, February 1989.

Stein, Isabel. Letter to the Editor. *Modern Maturity*, June/July 1989.

Wilder, Rachel. "Now the kids can rough it, too." *U.S. News and World Report*, April 3, 1989.

Schwartz, Joe. "What's left after taxes." *American Demographics*, November 1987.

Chapter 8

Bartos, Rena. *The Moving Target.* New York: Free Press, 1982.

Francese, Peter. "Women's Majority Milestones." *American Demographics*, September and October 1987.

Stipp, Horst H. "What is a Working Woman?" *American Demographics*, July 1988.

Castro, Janice. "She Calls All the Shots." *Time*, July 4, 1988.

Schwartz, Joe. "Who's the Boss." *American Demographics*, April 1988.

"Women and the New Enterprise Ethic." *Sky Magazine*, April 1988.

"How Single Women Spend." *American Demographics*, April 1988.

Dychtwald, Ken. *Age Wave*.

"Betting on Yourself." *Lear's*, March/April 1988.

Chapter 9

Edmondson, Brad. "Conquer the Baby Bust." *American Demographics*, September 1987.

"The Ways of Youth." *American Demographics*, May 1988.

Kaplan, Deborah. "Make Way, Boomers, here comes the Baby Busters." *Detroit Free Press*, February 8, 1987.

Smith, Nancy. "In the shadow of boomers." *The Oregonian*, July 30, 1989.

The Roper Organization. "The Baby Bust: A Return to 'Normal'?" *The Public Pulse*, November 1989.

Russell, Cheryl. "Trouble Ahead." *American Demographics*, March 1990.

"Baby Bust Incomes." *American Demographics*, October 1987.

"Teens Tune Out TV." *American Demographics*, March 1988.

Communication Research Associates Inc. "Which TV Spots Teens Like." *Public Relations Reports...Media Relations/Video Monitor*, Silver Spring, Maryland, 1988.

Part 3

Chapter 10

Naisbitt, John and Patricia Aburdene. *Megatrends 2000*. New York: William Morrow & Co, 1990.

Waldrop, Judith and Thomas Exter. "What the 1990 Census will Show." *American Demographics,* January 1990.

"Growth Around the USA." Survey by Arthur Andersen. *Inc.,* February 1990.

Naisbitt, John. *Megatrends.* New York: Warner Books, 1984.

Investments for Today and Tomorrow. The Kiplinger Washington Letter, Washington, D.C., 1990.

The Roper Organization. *The Public Pulse* 2, no. 1 (1988).

Ostroff, Jeff. *Outstanding Business Opportunities in a Graying America.* PrimeLife Marketing Division of the Data Group, Inc., Plymouth Meeting, PA, 1989.

The Kiplinger Washington Letter, February 16, 1990.

Farnsworth Riche, Martha. "The Consumers of the '90s." *The Numbers News,* January 1990.

Filips, Janet. "Looking into the '90s." *The Oregonian,* December 31, 1989.

Chapter 11

Rose, Matthew. "The Cocooning of America?" *Direct Marketing,* February 1990.

Dychtwald, Ken. *Age Wave.*

Edmondson, Brad. "Inside the Empty Nest." *American Demographics,* November 1987.

Kelly, Tom. "A Woman's Place is in the Home Remodeling Business." *Oregon Business,* December 1988.

Scanlan, Robert. "The Trends of the 1990s." *Oregon Business,* February 1989.

"Solving the Empty Nest Syndrome." *Direct Marketing,* December 1989.

Mankiw, N. Gregory and David N. Weil. *The Baby Boom, The Baby Bust, and the Housing Market.* Working Paper #2794, National Bureau of Economic Research, Inc., December 1988.

Schauer, Susan. "American Dream Getting Deferred." *Enterprise Courier*, Oregon City, OR, April 18, 1989.

Hart, B. Leslie. "3.45 million kitchens & 5.65 million baths in nation's remodeling." *Kitchen & Bath Business*, January 1989.

"Sinking the Money." *Research Alert*, August 8, 1989.

Wiener, Daniel P. "On the Home Front." *US News & World Report*, December 25, 1989/January 1, 1990.

Meehan, John, and David Zigas et al. "The Real Estate Slump: No End in Sight." *Business Week*, January 22, 1990.

"Housing prices falling down?" *Research Alert*, November 17, 1989.

MASCO Annual Report, Detroit, MI 1989.

Saunders, Dinah and Mark Smith. "Extras alluring for homebuyer." *The Oregonian*, January 27, 1990.

Hizenrath, David. "Age, demographics shifting to affect demand for housing." *The Oregonian*, December 10, 1989.

Hall, Trish. "Home turns into sweet workplace." *The Oregonian*, December 12, 1989.

Cutler, Blayne. "Getting Ahead in Slippers." *American Demographics*, February 1990.

Chapter 12

Jones, Landon, Y. *Great Expectations.*

Dychtwald, Ken. *Age Wave.*

Russell, Cheryl. "Class Boom." *American Demographics*, November 1987.

Naisbitt, John. *Megatrends.*

"Summer 1989." Newsletter from Louis Phillips and Associates, Athens, GA.

Elmer-Dewitt, Philip. "Plugging in." *The Oregonian,* February 27, 1990.

"Begin a new lifetime." No. 7 in a series to advertisers, *Modern Maturity,* 1989.

Edmondson, Brad. "Why Adult Education is Hot." *American Demographics,* February 1988.

Graham, Ellen. "High-Tech Training." *The Wall Street Journal,* February 9, 1990.

Charlier, Marj. "Back to Basics." *The Wall Street Journal,* February 9, 1990.

"Continuing Education." *Inc.,* February 1990.

"Personal Computer Consumer Software Sales Up 26% in 1988." Press Release from Software Publishers Association, Washington, D.C., March 13, 1989.

"The Home Library." *Research Alert,* July 21, 1989.

Chapter 13

"Hotline." *Inc.,* March 1990.

Altman, Lawrence K. and Elisabeth Rosenthal. "Doctors in Distress." *The Oregonian,* February 25, 1990.

"More Women MDs." *Parents,* 1988.

"Spending—sometimes income doesn't matter." *The Numbers News,* January 1990.

Findlay, Steven and Joanne Silberner. "Costs and Cures." *U.S. News & World Report,* December 25, 1989/January 1, 1990.

"The AIDS Trade." *American Demographics,* January 1990.

Rapp, Stan. "Health-care innovations we can learn from." *Direct Marketing*, December 1989.

Beck, Joan. "Effects of Alzheimer's cast ominous shadow." *The Oregonian*, November 22, 1989.

Thomas, Richard and William Sehnert. "The Dual Health-Care Market." *American Demographics*, April 1989.

Roark, Anne C. "U.S. growing health-conscious." *The Oregonian*, October 11, 1989.

"The Fit & the Fat." A Prevention Report on Patterns in Health Behavior. *Prevention Magazine*, Emmaus, PA October 1989.

Schultz, Mark. "City of Battling Hospitals." *American Demographics*, May 1989.

Kiester, Jr., Edwin. "Waking Up to Elder Care." *New Choices*, February 1989.

"The American Diet Market." (chart) *The Oregonian*, January 22, 1990.

Doyle, Thomas B. "Survival of the Fittest." *American Demographics*, May 1989.

The Roper Organization. "Health Club Patronage is Up." *The Public Pulse*, March 1989.

"Fit in Florida." *American Demographics*, May 1989.

Ostroff, Jeff. "An Aging Market." *American Demographics*, May 1989.

Ostroff, Jeff. *Outstanding Business Opportunities in a Graying America.*

Chapter 14

Clarke, Jay. "Club Med family resorts go upscale in '90s." *The Oregonian*, January 28, 1990.

"Future Travel Log." *Research Alert*, November 3, 1989.

Maves, Jr., Norm. "Destinations for the Decade: The Big Three." *The Oregonian*, December 31, 1989.

The Roper Organization. "Hotel/Motel Guests Increase." *The Public Pulse*, March 1989.

"The Un-cruised." *Research Alert*, November 17, 1989.

"Have Family, will Travel." *Research Alert*, November 17, 1989.

Dunn Rawn, Cynthia. "Marketing Spare Time." *American Demographics*, March 1990.

"A Slice of Golf Life." *Research Alert*, November 3, 1989.

"Hobbies & Households." *Research Alert*, July 21, 1989.

Russell, Cheryl. "Everyone's Gone to the Moon." *American Demographics*, February 1990.

McCarthy, Michael J. "Restaurants Search for Winning Recipes." *The Wall Street Journal*, January 29, 1990.

Charlier, Marj. "Maverick of Dinner Houses Faces Spaghetti Shoot-Out." *The Wall Street Journal*, January 29, 1990.

"ETCETERA." *American Demographics*, March 1990.

"Middle-Aged Daredevils." *American Demographics*, February 1990.

Henk, Dianne. " 'Boo' go the Boomers." *The Journal News*, Rockland County, NY, October 29, 1988.

Rothenberg, Randall. "Nostalgia becomes a craze of the present." *The Oregonian*, December 10, 1989.

"High Frequency." *American Demographics*, March 1990.

The Roper Organization. "VCRs: Penetration Near Complete Among Affluent." *The Public Pulse*, March 1989.

"Women Viewing to Network Sports." New York: BBDO Media Research Dept., October 1989.

Gonzales, Monica. "Business Reports—Art Mart." *American Demographics*, July 1988.

Dunn, Stephen. "Reach Out and Touch Donors." *Fund Raising Management*, March 1988.

Lacayo, Richard. "A Surging New Spirit." *Time*, July 11, 1988.

"Entertainers." *Eastern Review*, January 1989.

Ostroff, Jeff. "An Aging Market." *American Demographics*, May 1989.

Dychtwald, Ken. *Age Wave*.

Charboneau, F. Jill. "No Time for Art." *American Demographics*, January 1989.

Chapter 15

Ostroff, Jeff. *Outstanding Business Opportunities in a Graying America*.

"The Preferred Stash." *American Demographics*, April 1988.

Luciano, Lani. "'Pre-Retirees' Long on Hope, Short on Readiness." *Money*, March 1990.

"Cashing Checks is a Growth Business." *Oregon Business*, February 1989.

"A Boomer Economy." *Research Alert*, August 8, 1989.

"ETCETERA." *American Demographics*, December 1989.

Stern, Linda. "Saving seen as next wave for boomers." *The Oregonian*, November 10, 1989.

Dentzer, Susan. "How we will live." *US News & World Report*, December 25, 1989/January 1, 1990.

Tripp, Julie. "Consultant says clients' attitudes add up to 'money personality'." *The Oregonian*, September 18, 1988.

Farnsworth Riche, Martha. "Holistic Marketing." *American Demographics*, January 1990.

Green, Andrea. "Retail Banking's Mad, Mad Scramble for Market Share." *Bankers Monthly*, September 1989.

Dychtwald, Ken. *Age Wave*.

Tripp, Julie. "Sandwich generation feels pinch." *The Oregonian*, May 21, 1989.

Cohen, Robert. "American women's nests rarely empty, study finds." *The Oregonian*, May 11, 1989.

Schwartz, Joe. "Wampum Woes." *American Demographics*, May 1989.

Edmondson, Brad. "Inside the Empty Nest." *American Demographics*, November 1987.

"Future banks to diversify with wide array of services." *East Portland-Clackamas County Edition, Senior Tribune*, November 1989.

Hayes, Christopher L. "Financial Security: What Every Woman Must Know." *McCall's*, October 1989.

Part 4

Chapter 16

Alsop, Ronald. "Brand Loyalty is Rarely Blind Loyalty." *The Wall Street Journal*, October 19, 1989.

"Me: The Next Generation." *Research Alert*, November 3, 1989.

"Tomorrow's Consumer." *American Demographics*, July 1988.

"Buy now, or save later." *Research Alert*, November 3, 1989.

"Selling Images: Brands and Stores." *Research Alert*, November 3, 1989.

"Brands of Loyalty." *Research Alert*, August 8, 1989.

"Car-rumba!" *Research Alert*, August 8, 1989.

Hazelton, Lynette. "Food Fights." *Business Journal of New Jersey*, May 1989.

Deveny, Kathleen. "Middle-Price Brands Come Under Siege." *The Wall Street Journal*, April 2, 1990.

Chapter 17

Huntsinger, Jerry. "Direct Mail: Sweeping Changes Since 1969." *Fund Raising Management*, April 1989.

Naisbitt, John. *Megatrends*.

"Packaging: more of less." *Research Alert*, November 17, 1989.

Gerstman, Richard. "Packaging in the 1990s." Speech at East-Pack 1988.

"Coupon Craze Cools." *American Demographics*, October 1988.

"Get the Message." *American Demographics*, December 1989.

"Campus Mail" and "Mature Mail." *American Demographics*, March 1988.

Schlosberg, Jeremy. "The Write Stuff." *American Demographics*, September 1989.

"Hispanics Rank High on Coupon Redemption Scale." *Direct Marketing*, September 1988.

"Hispanic Clippers." *American Demographics*, March 1988.

"In the lead." *Parade Magazine*, February 18, 1990.

Pickholz, Jerome W. "The End of the World." *Direct Marketing*, September 1988.

Turchiano, Francesca. "The (Un)Malling of America." *American Demographics*, April 1990.

Chapter 18

Naisbitt, John. *Megatrends.*

Kotler, Philip. *Marketing for Nonprofit Organizations.* New York: Prentice Hall, 1975.

Nichols, Judith E. "Personality Theory Weds Programs." *Fund Raising Management,* October 1986.

Chapter 19

Varadarajan, P. Rajan and Anil Memon. "Cause Related Marketing: A Coalignment of Marketing Strategy and Corporate Philanthropy." *American Marketing Association Journal.*

Greene, Stephen G. "Business Leaders Back Idea of Corporate Philanthropy, but Question Likelihood of Growth Soon, Survey Finds." *The Chronicle of Philanthropy,* October 25, 1988.

Sterne, Larry. "Market Yourself." *NonProfit Times,* January 1989.

Reiss, Alvin. "Just how far down is the bottom line." *Fund Raising Management,* August 1989.

Swenson, Chester A. "How to Speak to Hispanics." *American Demographics,* February 1990.

Stehle, Vince. "A Latter-Day Matchmaker Tries to Pair Arts Organizations with Corporations Interested in Gifts and Public Relations." *Chronicle of Philanthropy,* September 5, 1989.

"Study of Cause-Related Marketing." Independent Sector, 1988.

Schwartz, Joe. "Frito Parks." *American Demographics,* February 1989.

Williams, Roger. "What hath Geldof Wrought?" *Foundation News,* January/February 1987.

Westerman, Marty. "Death of the Frito Bandito." *American Demographics,* March 1989.

Kotkin, Joel. "Selling to the New America." *Inc.*, July 1987.

"Spiegel Catalog aids Charities." *Fund Raising Management*, January 1990.

Stoute, Lenny. "Tour de Force Paul McCartney." *Vis A Vis*, April 1990.

Makower, Joel. "The Green Revolution." *Vis A Vis*, April 1990.

Schwartz, Joe. "Earth Day Today." *American Demographics*, April 1990.

Robbins, Elaine. "Doing the Right Thing." *Vis A Vis*, April 1990.

"Guidelines developed for Cause-Related Marketing." *Non-Profit Times*, January 1988.

Part 5

Chapter 20

Morris, Michele. "The new breed of leaders." *Working Woman*, March 1990.

"Why She Started the Business." *Inc.*, April 1990.

"Lunch." Frances Lear interview with Lester Korn. *Lear's*, March 1990.

Rogers, Elaine. "Women & The New Enterprise Ethic." *Sky Magazine*, April 1988.

Schwartz, Joe. "Who's the Boss?" *American Demographics*, April 1988.

"Women in Franchising." *Inc.*, April 1990.

Cadden, Vivian. "The Force of the Future." *Working Mother*, May 1989.

Brandt, Ellen. "Could You Run a Business with Your Spouse." *Parade Magazine*, June 4, 1989.

Cook, Dan. "The Silent Minority." *California Business*, October 1989.

Carey, John. "The Pepsi Generation Heads for the Corner Office." *Business Week*, September 25, 1989.

Jones, Chuck. "Small business good activity for retired seniors." *Senior Tribune of Portland*, January 2, 1990.

Chapter 21

Sandroff, Ronni. "Why it Won't Be Business as Usual." *Working Woman*, January 1990.

Wolf, Stephen M. "Editorial Opinion." *Vis A Vis*, June 1989.

Edmondson, Brad. "Help Desperately Wanted." *American Demographics*, January 1990.

Exter, Thomas. "Demographic Forecasts: Job Applicants." *American Demographics*, November 1989.

DeVenuta, Karin. "Education Openers." *The Wall Street Journal*, February 9, 1990.

Charen, Mona. "Intergenerational day care may unburden women caregivers." *The Oregonian*, March 19, 1990.

Rothstein, Frances R. "Tomorrow's Hot Benefit: Elder Care." Letter to the Editor. *Working Woman*, March 1990.

Swasy, Alecia and Carol Hymowitz. "The Workplace Revolution." *The Wall Street Journal*, February 9, 1990.

Karr, Albert R. "To Have & Have Not." *The Wall Street Journal*, February 9, 1990.

Evangelauf, Jean. "Demand for College-Educated Workers May Outstrip Supply in 1990s." *Chronicle of Higher Education*, January 23, 1990.

"The '90s' Men lacking education may face trouble." *The Oregonian*, December 31, 1990.

Friedman, Dana and Wendy Gray. *A Life Cycle Approach to Family Benefits and Policies*, Perspective No. 19, New York: The Conference Board.

The Numbers News, February 1990.

Beck, Joan. "Workplace changes show increasing value of women." *The Oregonian*, October 12, 1989.

Russell, Cheryl. "Taking the Cure." *American Demographics*, March 1989.

Cadden, Vivian. "The Force of the Future." *Working Mother*, May 1989.

Brophy, Bethy. "Corporate Nannies for a New Decade." *US News & World Report*, December 25, 1989/January 1, 1990.

Moskowitz, Milton and Carol Townsend. "The Best Companies for Working Mothers." *Working Mother*, October 1989.

Bush, President George. Inaugural Address. January 20, 1989.

Copeland, Lennie. "Valuing Diversity: Making the Most of Cultural Differences at the Workplace" and "Valuing Diversity: Pioneers and Champions of Change." *Personnel*, June/July 1988.

Nelton, Sharon. "Meet Your New Work Force." *Nation's Business*, July 1988.

Braham, Jim. "No, You Don't Manage Everyone the Same." *Industry Week*, February 6, 1989.

Diversity: A Source of Strength. DuPont Report. 1989.

Volunteerism and Charitable Giving: The National Outlook for 1989. Survey by the Marist Institute for Public Opinion, Poughkeepsie, New York, January/February 1989.

Sewell, Jr., Marshall. "Retired Power: Putting it to work." *Fund Raising Management*, December 1988.

Guidelines for Outreach to Minority Populations (ARC 7000) and *Hispanic Outreach Guidelines (ARC 7007)*. American Red Cross, August 1987.

The Chivas Regal Report on Working Americans: Emerging Values for the 1990s. Conducted by Research & Forecasts, New York, 1989.

"The Golden Benefit." *Research Alert*, August 4, 1989.

"Health in Business." Supplement to *The Business Journal*, January 1989.

Braus, Patricia. "A Workout for the Bottom Line." *American Demographics*, October 1989.

Olivero, Magaly. "The Corporate Sabbatical: A Win Win Approach." *Working Woman*, June 1989.

Kohut, Andrew and Linda DeStefano. "Modern Employees Expect More From Their Careers; Job Dissatisfaction Particularly High Among the Young." *The Gallup Poll News Service*, September 4, 1989.

The Roper Organization. "Job Satisfaction Hits 15-Year Low; New Era for Working America." *The Public Pulse*, March 1989.

Corporate and Employee Response to caring for the Elderly. Survey by *Fortune* and John Hancock Financial Services, 1989.

Hunt, Ann. "Caretaker burnout." *The Oregonian*, December 10, 1989.

McDermott, Judy. "Essence of Caring." *The Oregonian*, December 17, 1989.

Chapter 22

"United States of America." *Research Alert*, August 4, 1989.

America in the 21st Century: A Demographic Overview. Report from Population Reference Bureau, Washington, D.C., 1989.

Index